The Basic Guide to Pricing Your Craftwork

With Profitable Strategies for Recordkeeping, Cutting Costs, Time & Workspace Management, Plus Tax Advantages of Your Craft Business

James Dillehay

from Warm Snow Publishers
Torreon, New Mexico

More books by this author:
The Basic Guide to Selling Arts and Crafts
The Basic Guide to Selling Crafts on the Internet
Directory of Grants for Crafts & How to Write a Winning Proposal
Overcoming the 7 Devils That Ruin Success
Your Guide to Ebook Publishing Success

© 2007 by Warm Snow Publishers

First Edition

Published by:
Warm Snow Publishers
P.O. Box 75
Torreon, NM 87061

ISBN: 0-9629923-2-1
Library of Congress Cat. Card No.: 97-090001

Printed and bound in the United States of America

Printed on acid-free papers

This book is dedicated to my father, James Dillehay, Sr., who grew up in the farming country of East Texas and later went on to build a successful business in retail. When I began pontificating on the question of pricing, I remembered a story he used to tell me about prices. One customer in the farmer's market once said to another about a farmer selling produce, "What he's a askin' and what he's a gittin' are two different things."

Contents

Introduction

One of the most often asked questions from craftpersons selling their work is *"How much should I charge?"* Whether you have been in business for some time, or you are just starting, this handbook will help you answer that question.

This guide gives you basic formulas for pricing your craftwork in selling retail or wholesale, how to use pricing strategies to increase sales, how to know if you are really making a profit, how to keep records, and how to manage your time and workspace to get the most profit out of every hour and increase productivity. In addition to learning about several tax advantages to your home based craft business, you'll learn ways to boost your daily available cash income.

We will take a look at how recordkeeping affects your overall business and marketing planning. You'll get a new perspective on the many diverse elements that make up what your business is about. And you'll discover how all of these elements interrelate.

It's a fact that many crafters do not charge enough for their work. I certainly didn't, when I began selling. This often comes from a failure to realize the value of our work not only to ourselves as artisans, but also to the customers who support the craft industry economically through purchases.

Like many, you may prefer a simple formula to plug in all the numbers and come up with a workable price. You'll find several formulas in these chapters and much more.

You'll also learn why you should look at your prices at regular intervals. The cost of living goes up. What prices the market will bear changes with time and local economic conditions.

This handbook will help you arrive at a working knowledge of at least two things: the actual cost of your craftwork and the selling price you ask for it. You'll be able to look back on how you arrived at your current situation and successfully use that data to plan where you want to go.

The real growth, fun and eventual profits come from realizing how much power you have to affect important questions that determine the success of your business: *How much is the customer willing to pay?* or *What is my craftwork worth to them?*

In this book you will learn techniques to increase the value customers place on your craftwork. You will also see how raising that perceived value will boost your profit margins, increase your market share, and provide opportunities for even more creativity in your work.

You can benefit right now from applying the formulas and strategies presented here. There's enough material in this book to give your business a strategic tune-up, while hopefully giving you a new and larger perspective on the way you look at and feel about your venture.

There's even a chapter on tax advantages of a small home based business. Here you'll find legal ways to cut your tax bills and boost your net income.

If you are really interested in surviving as a craft artist, you should know that the process of gathering the information that enables you to come up with a correct pricing policy is the same activity that gives you a thermometer to measure the overall health of your business. It's all part of the big picture.

Even if you use all the formulas found in these pages and anywhere else, the prices you first come to apply in your craft business may soon change. That is because profitable pricing ultimately comes from testing and measuring.

Gather all the facts from the recordkeeping practices described in this book and look at what the market says about craftwork similar to yours. The correct price will be one that feels right and works to bring you maximum profits.

You'll love the results of knowing exactly where your business stands at any given moment and how you can use your knowledge to achieve both personal and financial goals.

To be successful as a professional craftperson, you will need to apply some amount of discipline in keeping records. Yes, that means making a few extra efforts. But just imagine those small efforts yielding big sales and maximum profits starting today.

Chapter 1
Basic Pricing 101

"We can tell our values by
looking at our checkbook stubs."
- Gloria Steinem

Pricing means that you charge for your products based on values. There are two sets of values to consider. The first is how much the customer values your work. The second is how much you value your work. Both values are based on benefits. What is the benefits your customer will derive from acquiring your craftwork? What are the benefits you derive from being successful at your craft business?

You can upgrade both values right now and see immediate returns in increased sales and profits.

Motivating yourself

Remind yourself every morning of what you expect to gain from having your own craft business. Write down your goals and dreams. You want more personal freedom. You want to work when, where and how you choose. You desire more income. You want to express yourself creatively.

These desires motivated you to become self-employed. Your dreams, if you keep reminding yourself of them, will keep you involved in your business despite longer hours, often less pay, and unexpected challenges.

An excellent tool for motivating yourself and upgrading the value you set on being in business is to create a "dream book." Collect photographs from magazines that portray those things you want in vivid imagery. Paste these photos on the pages of a blank book such as a photo album.

For instance, you might want a new car. Look through a magazine with pictures of the exact car you want. Cut it out and paste it into your book. You could also do this with images of far-off places you wish to travel to. Find photos of families having fun together. Whatever you want in life, find a picture and place in your book.

By looking at your dream book frequently, you remind yourself of your values and desires. Your subconscious will begin to help you act in ways which will bring your dreams into reality.

> *"If one is lucky, a solitary fantasy can totally transform one million realities."* - Maya Angelou

Every day, spend five or ten minutes visualizing having already achieved your own goals. What does it feel like to own your life, to have money to do what you want, to take off work when you want more time with the family.

If you build such a mental image of yourself as already a success on the center stage of your mind, you will begin to do all the little things necessary to achieve those desires. That includes taking a little time every week to keep records; then spending a few moments to analyze them to see where your business is headed.

If you have needs and values that motivate you, you can believe your customers can be motivated, too. Part of reaching your sales goals will come from educating customers how your products will fulfill their needs.

What motivates customers

In my book, *The Basic Guide to Selling Arts & Crafts,* I explain the psychological theory of human motivation which says that everyone is motivated by a set of needs. In summary, those basic human needs are freedom from fear, good health, emotional comfort, more money, being popular, convenience, entertainment, someone to love, time, sexual fulfillment, pride, physical comfort, warmth, attractiveness, prestige, and so on.

Evaluate your products against the list and see if they help meet any of the basic needs. A handmade quilt or bedspread might keep you warm, bring value as an heirloom, be worthy of pride, and convenient to use.

What you are selling then, is the answer to your customer's needs. Seen in this light, the pricing question then becomes one of determining how much value people place on getting their needs met.

I noticed at craft shows occasionally a customer asked me about how long it took to make or what materials were in a piece they were admiring. Most of the time, however, the person wanted and needed to know how the piece looked on them in front of a mirror. Their second concern was how much it cost. If my price was not out of line with what the average market price was for that type of product, I usually made a sale.

Advertisers and marketing experts make use of human motivational triggers all the time when designing promotional material. The idea is to move a person to buy a product by stimulating one or more basic need. However, it's important to note that even though people have a wide range of needs, it is really what they want that makes them act. When you become aware that you are in fact providing the fulfillment of what people want, you will experience a brighter dawn in all of your marketing results.

Therefore, let your packaging and promotional material remind your customers of benefits they will receive upon becoming the proud owner of one of your pieces.

This theory of meeting the customer's desires is opposite almost all beginning craft sellers' thinking and perhaps one of the more difficult barriers to success. A simple reminder is that customers buy products based on their wants and needs, not yours. When all other circumstances are equal, customer benefit oriented selling will almost always give you the competitive edge.

Value of your work

New crafters are often overly modest about charging enough for their craftwork in the start-up phase of their business. They ask themselves, *"Who am I to charge so much?"* I started out that way, too. It's quite natural to feel that way, even though it works against you.

When I was first learning to weave, I wove a sampler scarf using many different patterns, yarns, and colors my teacher gave me to experiment with. It was a great feeling when only two weeks after beginning (this same piece would now take me two hours) I was ready to cut the finished piece off the loom. As it happened, a friend walked by soon afterward and saw it draped over my loom. It was my first commercial display. She saw the scarf, fell in love with it, and said she wanted to buy it.

Wow! Was I excited! The only problem was I had no idea what to charge. After all, she was a friend and I was *only* a beginner. Meekly, I said *"How about $20."* She said okay and that was my first sale.

That spur of the moment pricing decision wasn't based on appropriate value. I didn't stop to figure how many hours I had worked or the cost of the materials. Of course, I knew I was in the learning phase and that my labor time would decrease when I got more experience. Still, I should have checked with my teacher before quoting such a low price. I learned later my friend would have paid three times as much for that scarf which she still treasures years after her purchase. She valued the piece for its beauty, originality, and because I was an artist.

Increasing perceived value

Perceived value is the worth the customer places on a given purchase like my friend just mentioned. Newcomers almost always underprice their craft products thinking they will attract more buyers. This process, however, is actually self-defeating because the artisan undermines the perceived value of their handicraft. If a piece isn't selling, you can increase its apparent value by various means. One way is to use more expensive materials and emphasize the exclusiveness of the finished piece.

I once wove a series of shawls with cotton and mohair yarns. Pricing them at $65 each. For several months, they just didn't sell. I replaced the hangtags with new ones emphasizing that the pieces contained "pure Angora mohair" and raised the price to $85. They all sold the first time on display. This success inspired me to make more pieces emphasizing the expensive materials which also sold at the higher price.

Accenting benefits over features

Another effective marketing and pricing strategy to enhance value is to stress how a product will benefit your customer. The customer is really shopping for benefits.

There is an important difference between features and benefits. For example, these next three statements speak about features:

14

"This wool and mohair jacket is handmade from all naturally dyed yarn."

"These rag rugs are woven with long lasting, durable materials."

"This rocker is solid oak and handcarved."

The customer is almost always less interested in *what it is* then *what it will do for them*. Remember what they are really buying is the answer to some need or desire.

Note how changing the above statements to emphasize benefits tells the customer how they will benefit, thus increasing the perceived value:

"This wool and mohair jacket will keep you warm on those cool nights."

"Your one-of-a-kind rag rug will last you a long time. You'll be able to walk on it comfortably for years."

"This heirloom, handmade rocker will increase in value over time as a collector's dream."

Packaging and promotional material

Another way of increasing perceived value is to make use of elaborate packaging techniques. This includes employing descriptive hang tags, price tags, brochures, ribbons, fancy boxes, or wrapping.

If your tags are becoming worn from handling, replace them to keep the appearance that products are new. A worn out tag sends a signal to customers, *"this piece isn't selling, why should I buy it?"*

People today often buy the packaging of a product before the contents. Write and design hangtags and brochures that tell a story about your craft's heritage. Does it require unique skills? You can tell people the benefits they will enjoy from your craft products. You can package your work in elaborate boxes or wrapping that speaks to the desires of the customer saying *"Collectible. I need to own this."*

A fiber artist I know of used this technique to build an incredible demand for his work. He produced handwoven scarves from hand-dyed silk yarns. The quality of his work was exceptional and would have sold for a good price on their own merits. However, he also designed a beautiful box with an accompanying booklet explaining the history of weaving to go along with each scarf.

The cost of the scarves before the box was $75. By adding attractive packaging, he increased the retail price to $95. This is an example of how customers were encouraged by the artist to perceive a higher value.

Wouldn't you agree it would be worth spending an additional $4 to upgrade a product's perceived value through packaging if you could earn an extra $20 in profit?

And extra profit isn't the only benefit here. With this craftperson's unique packaging and exceptional product, he captured new markets, increased his name recognition, and experienced phenomenal growth in his sales.

Art or craft on display does inspire a certain amount of value in customers' minds on its own. Even so, you can build on that intrinsic value. You can create perception of a higher value and therefore command a higher price.

The same equation sometimes works in reverse, too. The price of your craft products affects the way your work is perceived.

For instance, a higher priced item as compared to similar work by other crafters may indicate quality and equality with products deemed special by your customers. By experimenting, you may find that the higher price does not affect sales adversely. In that instance, you would not need to lower your prices even if you could afford to.

If customers think a product isn't worth the price, they won't buy. The flip side is when they think your product has exceptional value, you can charge more.

Relating price to craft sales

When we are new in the business, we believe that pricing is the only obstacle to customers making a purchase. We imagine there is a direct one-to-one relationship between prices and sales. This is not always true. Price becomes important to the buyer only when that customer cannot perceive any difference in your work and another crafter's, that is, when perceived value is not a consideration. For example, say there are twelve booths at a craft fair selling leather belts of similar construction. A customer then begins looking for the cheapest belt. If you are the only booth showing leather belts, price becomes secondary to the customer's decision. If you hold the view that price is the main reason people buy, you ignore the power of increasing perceived value.

What makes your work different

After you have made it clear to customers how they will benefit from owning your work, you can make known its exceptional features. Differentiating your work from similar artists is the next vital requirement in surviving in the marketplace. Don't ignore those features of your craft that make yours a little different, a little better in the eyes of your customers.

Communicate through product design or packaging or informational tags the real strengths of your craftwork. For instance, make it known you use the best or perhaps rare materials in construction. Maybe it's important that you do every single step of the craft by hand or with traditional hand tools. Do you come from a long line of craftworkers in your family? Are you one of the few artisans in a craft that is no longer practiced widely? Is your studio located near a place of historical significance?

If you don't tell customers why your work is better, they will not guess.

Before, I mentioned a fiber artist who created great packaging around his work. His boxes were so different and so exquisite, it became apparent to customers his work was also unique and desirable above the competition.

Producing craft unlike anyone else's is one of the most enjoyable aspects of making and selling your work. Let your customers know why your work is original.

Target the collector customer

Creating a series of work can add value to your prices. For instance you could produce a limited or numbered series designed in a unique theme such as tigers, or penguins, or rainbows, or dragons. Shoppers will become "collector" customers with less concern for the price you ask as the value of owning another in an original series of your work. Your reputation or regard as an artist will help you develop a mailing list of these collector customers over time.

Here's another value enhancing tip to attract collectors. Lore Wills, a fiber artist in New Mexico names her elegant, high priced pieces. Lore calls one of her $700 coats, "Begonia Dreams," another is named "Sage Sunsets."

Provide additional customer benefits

There are some services you can offer that will favor increasing your sales even if you face a lot of competition. For instance, you may do custom work for special customers and charge extra.

You can provide additional services instead of charging a lower price for your work. Consider that many crafters have found more success by raising their prices. They employ elaborate or well thought out packaging and promotional material as already mentioned. They may offer better customer service like accepting credit cards, gift wrapping, or exhibiting in an elegantly designed booth display.

In selling direct to customers yourself, success more often depends on how well you demonstrate or display superior craftsmanship and impeccable service than how low your prices are. To the typical craft consumer, prices are not the dominant factor in buying decisions. If the customer 'needs' to own one of your pieces, they'll buy it.

In this chapter we have looked at how values affect pricing. When you upgrade the value you and your customers place on your work through promotional material and positioning, you will see a dramatic improvement in sales and profits.

Pricing is a dynamic, ongoing process. There is constant interaction between the prices you ask and your promotional and sales aids. Part of your marketing plan should include reexamining your prices periodically to learn if you could be getting higher prices through raising the perceived value of your work. Consider the following:

• Your projected image as an artisan/craftperson to attract customers.

- Your customers perceptions of their own needs and the anticipated benefits from buying your work.
- How sensitive your customers are to different prices.
- How your craftwork compares to other crafters in features and prices.
- How price changes actually affect your sales volume and profitability.
- Alternatives to changing prices such as increased service or reputation.

Pricing can be a strategic part of building a more competitive business. The next chapter shows you how to employ pricing as an added leverage to achieve bigger sales volume.

Chapter 2
Using Pricing Strategies

*"Results! Why, man, I have
gotten a lot of results. I know
several thousand things that
won't work."*   - Thomas Edison

This chapter will show you how to use pricing in specific circumstances to increase your market share. The situations where prices can change include: where you sell your work, the time of year, amount of competition, and the newness of your product. In many cases, you can use pricing to boost your sales. But like Thomas Edison trying to create a light bulb, the only way to really know what works is to test your prices and measure what happens.

Where you sell

You can charge more for your work in places where the economy is good or growing. On the other hand, if people are out of work, craft items will be an unlikely attraction. You have to go where the money is.

If your local area is financially depressed, this may mean traveling to shows in other states where jobs and disposable income are plentiful. Another solution is to place your work in shops, galleries, and craft malls in other areas around the country. You should also stay informed of trends in tourism so you can follow the money trail to states where craft sales are booming.

One way of getting a good picture of economies in states or areas you are considering selling to is by contacting your local SBA - Small Business Administration office or SBDC - Small Business Development Center.

Many offices will have on hand a copy of *Small Business Profiles*, an annual compilation of the latest economic and small business information for all states in the country. To locate an SBDC near you, call or write the lead center for your state listed in the appendix.

Small Business Profiles provides an overview of each state's economy such as new firms, business dissolutions, small business income, exports, and detailed data on the economy not available elsewhere.

For example, the 1995 *Small Business Profiles* stated that in New Mexico, employment in the state rose 8.4 percent in the last two years. In that same time, national employment rose only 3.9 percent. New Mexico unemployment decreased 1.5 percent from the previous year. That information indicates the state is experiencing economic growth.

You can also safeguard yourself from local economic conditions by using sales reps to reach more prosperous areas. You can exhibit at craft wholesale trade shows where buyers attend from all over the country. If your crafts and prices are appropriate, try selling through national mail order magazines and catalogs like *Hearth Song,* Robert Redford's *Sundance Collection, Country Sampler,* or *Better Homes & Gardens Crafts Showcase.* You might also consider selling through a cable home shopping channel like QVC. For more information on selling nationally, see *The Basic Guide to Selling Arts & Crafts.*

Positioning

Position your crafts in markets where customers arrive with a set of perceived values and price expectations already in their minds. For instance, display your goods at one of the better, juried fine art/craft show. Customers at these shows are willing and even expect to pay more than they would for mass produced items. Another example is getting your work featured in galleries along side high priced items. Mail order catalogs that features quality crafts like those mentioned above are another place where customers have expectations of a higher price range. Each market has its own loyal customers.

As you may have already found, different kinds of craft shows attract different groups of shoppers with whole different sets of preconceived notions about what they are looking for and how much they will spend.

In my beginning years, I once read a glowing review in a craft fair guide of a show in a city 600 miles from me. This guide did not, unfortunately, distinguish between the different kinds of shows reviewed or the average price range of items sold. I was still too new to know there are a variety of shows and how important it is to know what kinds of crafts are shown and what kind of crowd attends.

This particular show attracted country craft makers and country craft buyers expecting country craft prices. This would

Your craft items may reflect a hot consumer trend in other countries. To find out what's happening in the rest of the world, the Small Business Administration (SBA) produces Export Information System (XIS), a database of hot products and trends on 25 world trade markets, including growth statistics. For more information, contact: Office of International Trade, Small Business Admin., 409 Third St SW #6100, Washington DC 20416, (202)205-6720.

have been a terrific if I made country crafts, often priced between $5 and $50. But I didn't. I handwove garments and rugs. My average piece retailed for $150 while the average craft item at this show retailed for $30 or less. I sold almost nothing. There was one sale to a visitor from Germany who was someone's guest. He recognized the quality of my work without the preconceived set of values or price expectations most of the show's attendees arrived with. The very next weekend, we set up at an event in another town near the first in a juried show. This event brought in over $3,000 in sales and most of those were our best pieces. This juried event drew crowds who arrived expecting to find high end pieces.

Read as many different reviews of a fair as you can find. Talk to recent exhibitors. Be discriminating when selecting which shows to do. Find those shows which bring in customers looking for the type and price range of crafts you make. IT IS CRUCIAL that you find shows that match your work. In *The Basic Guide to Selling Arts & Crafts,* I devote an entire chapter on selecting the right shows for your craft and getting the most from them. Craft show performances can change quickly from year to year. Craft show guides that list and sometimes review shows are listed here.

Art and Craft News
P.O. Box 26624
Jacksonville, FL 32226
904-757-3913

The ArtFair SourceBook
1234 S. Dixie Hwy, #11
Coral Gables, FL 33146
800-358-2045

Crafter's Guide
1772 Red Lion Rd
Bear DE 19701

www.Craftmarketer.com

Craftmaster News
P.O. Box 39429
Downey, CA 90239
310-869-5882

The Crafts Fair Guide
PO Box 688
Corte Madera CA 94976
(800)871-2341

The Crafts Report
PO Box 1992
Wilmington, DE 19899
800-777-7098

Craft Show List
PO Box 161
Catasauqua PA 18032
610-264-5325

Hands On Guide
255 Cranston Crest
Escondido CA 92025
619-747-8206

Harris Rhodes List
Box 142
La Veta, CO 81055
719-742-3146

Renaissance Trader Magazine
P.O. Box 422
Riverside, CA, 92502

Southern Arts and Crafts (SAC)
PO Box 159
Bogalusa, LA 70429
800-825-3722

Sunshine Artists
3210 Dade Ave.
Orlando, FL 32804
Phone: (407) 228-9772

Pricing by market

Price your craft items at different amounts according to the market you are selling through. For instance, you would establish separate price schedules for craft show customers, stores or galleries, and catalog companies. Within each market, however, you should keep your prices consistent. That is, charge one store the same prices as all stores.

Seasonal pricing

Some types of crafts have seasonal sales swings. Clothing and accessories are examples. Christmas ornaments are another. If your work is susceptible to seasonal sales, look for additional items to sell at those seasons when your other sales fall off rather than marking down prices to move inventory.

Also look at markets like craft fairs or craft malls in geographical locations that might be more profitable for your seasonal work at other times of the year. For instance, during the winter, many people travel to Arizona and Florida for the season. Place your winter items in shops in these states during the cold months. During the summer months, these same winter pieces may sell in stores in the northern states.

Learn what months covers the tourist season for various shops around the country, especially those located in scenic places. Ask store owners what their busy times of the year are. If a store is in a popular tourist locale, you can often command higher prices. Refer to the shop buyer for pricing suggestions.

Lowballing

If you make country crafts, you could price all your items at the low end of average prices for craftwork in your media. You may sell more to cost-conscious buyers. This strategy is not recommended for high end crafts. Lowballing is much more effective with crafts priced from $5 to $50. If your craftwork sells from $5 to $50, setting a lower price for new products in a price range of $10 or less might help you build a loyal customer base before other crafters can enter the market. Your low prices may even discourage them from ever trying. However, if *you* can afford to make it and sell it at a low price, so can anyone else.

When traveling to craft shows, you can save money and get decent lodging in hostels ranging in price between $5 and $22 per night. Become a member of Hostelling International, 733 15th St. NW Suite 840, Washington DC 20013, (202)783-6161 for $25 and get access to over 5,000 hostels in the U.S. and around the world. If you like to camp while you're traveling to shows, see the guide, *Camp The U.S. For $5 Or Less* ($13.95) by Mary Helen & Shuford Smith at book-stores or call (800)243-0495. Includes thousands of inexpensive or free camp sites.

Newness has its price

When a product is new to the marketplace and you have been the fortunate one to introduce it, you can help recover your initial investment quickly by setting the price artificially high. Demand for the item will be driven by its benefits, features, and newness. Price is not near as important in the buying decision of new products as it is with familiar ones. When you come out with a new item and there is little competition, pricing can be based on maximum profit. You are selling to customers who are willing to own this product because of its unique features. This makes the new product a premium.

When more crafters are making similar pieces, the customer has many choices. When this happens, competition for customers will hinge on price or service value. If the product is familiar, not new, and requires little or no education, the price of the item will be more important to your customer than the service value.

If a craft item is new and requires consumer education, than customer service will be more important than price.

If you find items like yours in abundance at other crafters' booths, the best thing to do is to attempt to improve your work, make it stand out, or give service so that customers can clearly and effortlessly see the benefits of your product over the other crafters' products. Another strategy would be to improve your reputation or image with brochures, tags, and other promotional packaging.

Demand pricing

If you notice over time that demand is weakening and sales are declining, it may be time to lower your prices slightly. When demand increases again, raise your prices. Continue raising prices over time until you find customer resistance or sales decreasing.

Be willing to change your prices gradually. Try a given set of prices for a couple of shows or presentations until you learn how customers respond. If there's no resistance to the price you're asking, you can probably raise it. When sales drop off and there is no other apparent reasons, return to the price you used before the last raise. You should also be periodically shopping the craft marketplace to learn what other crafters are pricing for similar work.

You may find pieces selling in stores but not at art and craft shows, and vice versa. Many items simply don't sell in every market. But this doesn't mean the products won't sell elsewhere or that you should lower the price.

Making a price sound right

When placing price tags on items, even dollar figures are perceived as more elite. A discount store might tag an item at $24.95 and a gallery would price the same product at $25.00. My woven garments retail at $80, $125, $150, and $250. My large rugs sell for $500 to $800. If I asked $499.95, people would think I was being cheap.

When answering a customer who asks about the price, share the benefits or value of a piece before actually saying the price. The point here is not to avoid answering their question, but to explain to the customer what they will be getting before telling them what they must pay. Practice acting out this situation with a crafting

If you need help with marketing or running your business, turn to a free handbook from IBM called *The Small Business Resource Guide* with hundreds of resources listed. Send your request to IBM Corporation, C. Piebes, Mail Drop 325 -- Resource Guide, 1133 Westchester Ave, White Plains, NY 10604.

friend through role playing. Each takes a turn being the customer and then the seller. That way, you both build confidence in making a presentation with ease.

Loss-leader pricing

You may attract additional customers by pricing some of your pieces at cost or lower. Though you may actually lose money on a few pieces, this tactic can be used to bring in buyers for more profitable items. Say you advertise a packet of dried herbs and flowers for $2 a pound. These packets are displayed with your new line of handmade collector vases priced at $49, which is what you really want your customer to buy. Loss-leader pricing is especially effective in mail order sales when you are introducing a new product to your existing customers. In general though, mail order sales are often unprofitable unless the item you are selling is priced at least $25.

Competitive pricing

When you are up against many crafters with the same items you make, try lowering your prices for a short time. However, you don't want to lose so much money it puts you out of business.

Additionally, you can give more services than your competitors. Provide gift wrapping, free delivery in the city, credit card acceptance, or a lay-a-way plan. Lay-a-way is where the customer puts a deposit down, usually fifty percent. They then make payments on a monthly basis until the piece is payed off. You keep the item until the customer sends the final payment.

It is good to learn what other crafters in your media are charging for similar work. As mentioned before, you should probably make it a point to check their prices at least once every few months. If all your competitors are raising their prices, it may be time to increase yours, too.

Rush service pricing

Whenever a customer is in a hurry for a custom made piece or special order, quote a price that includes an extra markup for your inconvenience, say at least 10% more than the typical price would be. This is quite common in almost all other services and usually expected. For instance, if you go to a local printer and ask for a rush job, they quote you a price that is above the normal price.

Is the price too high or too low?

You might think an item isn't selling because it's overpriced. There is a tendency among new artisans to mark down their products in an attempt to help the situation. However, this usually fails to produce the desired result. Unless you have tried and failed to move a piece for several months at a given price, you make a mistake in lowering the price thinking it will sell better. Most new entrepreneurs believe this is true because we all grew up under the influence of mass marketing. If Wal-Mart is having a sale, everyone goes shopping.

The concept of mass marketing, though, is exactly opposite to the reason people buy handmade crafts. If your craft products are perceived as valuable to the shopper, you will probably find they are just as willing to pay $25 for a handmade item as they would pay $20. I have often found that a piece sold faster by raising the price, than by lowering it. This is because of the element of perceived value. Sometimes the customer sees 'cheap' on a lower price tag and rejects the work as inferior.

You might also want to supplement an inventory of higher price crafts with smaller craft items within a price range of $10 to

$20. At shows where sales of high-ticket pieces are slow, I have found offering a range of low priced items brings in some sales.

People are always looking to buy something. We live in a consumer society where spending money has become an unconscious, yet sometimes, very conscious need in many people. If what you are making isn't selling, it doesn't necessarily mean that price is the reason. You may need to experiment making new or different products until you find items people will buy.

Bargaining

Every crafter who has done a few shows has been approached at the booth by at least one customer who wants to bargain down prices. If you are new to the business, it's easy for a clever bargainer to get you to feel and speak apologetically about your pricing. Just remember to not take it personally. These types probably try to negotiate the price on everything else they buy, too, not just your work. In of itself, that's not a bad way to approach making a purchase.

But why should you apologize for charging what you do for your art or craft? You spent considerable time and money to produce your pieces and you should receive fair payment in return.

This doesn't mean you can't bargain. The question is whether you should. The more years you have in the business the more confidence you have that your prices are fair and the less likely you will adopt bargaining on a regular basis. You know that you don't sell everything at one show and that there will be other shows down the road.

> However you price your pieces, quality of the work should justify the price you are asking. Any product should be designed and completed with attention to all the details.

New exhibitors might think it better to sell pieces at a discount when the show is ending just to move more items. The problem is once you start agreeing to bargain with customers, and therefore encouraging them to bargain, you derail the value of your work in your own eyes as well as anyone happening to be looking on at the time. How will you answer the next customer who asks, *"you gave her a bargain, what are you going to do for me?"*

A better option is to have pieces with slight faults on hand at discounted prices. Have the discounted pieces tagged with the full price marked down. Show the bargainers your sale rack.

Another risk newcomers take when they drop their prices is they don't get fair return on what they have invested in the piece. To know precisely what it costs you to make and sell your work, the next chapter provides the minimum price you must get to recover all your expenses.

Chapter 3
The Pricing Formula

*"As far as the laws of
mathematics refer to reality, they
are not certain, and as far as
they are certain, they do not refer
to reality."*   - Albert Einstein

Unlike in Einstein's theoretical mathematics and unlike in our own imaginations, you can identify with certainty realistic numbers for what it costs to make your craftwork. Once you know what it costs to produce an item and you have become familiar with all the pricing strategies we have talked about so far, you can arrive at the right price to ask. Go through the procedures in this book at least once a year to see if your prices still work to recover all your expenses.

You may be selling your work in several different kinds of markets like gift shops, home parties, craft shows, galleries, or through catalogs. In terms of pricing, these can all be separated into two categories, retail and wholesale.

Retail and wholesale prices

Retail price is what you ask for a piece when you are selling direct to the customer. Examples of places you might sell retail include art and craft shows, home parties, by mail order, or from your studio or retail store.

Wholesale price is what you ask for items you sell to someone else who in turn marks up the price and then sells it to their customers. For instance, stores, galleries, and catalogs would all be considered wholesale markets.

The new crafter may not yet be concerned with the difference between selling products retail like at craft fairs and selling wholesale to shops. However almost every crafter eventually encounters a shop buyer who suddenly appears in front of the booth at a craft fair and asks if you sell your work to stores. She wants to know your wholesale prices, payment terms, and when you can deliver. Are you ready with the answers?

Knowing if you can afford to sell wholesale profitably, can open new markets and bring in more income when show sales dip, fade, or dry up. Some crafters begin their business selling retail at craft fairs and then open up enough wholesale accounts that they can then stay home and work while the stores do the selling.

By analyzing your sales as explained later in Chapters 6 and 7, you might find that you make about the same profit selling at craft fairs compared to store sales at wholesale prices. Imagine the difference in your home life if you found you could make just as much money staying home and selling wholesale as you did traveling and selling retail at craft fairs every two or three weeks, twenty or thirty times a year. Wouldn't that be worth a little time spent recording your sales and expenses?

It isn't difficult to sell both through wholesale and retail channels as long as you keep the distinction between wholesale and retail pricing clear. You can price your work to sell at craft fairs or home parties by staying within the average market price. However, if you are selling to stores, you absolutely have to know the minimum or floor price to ask, discussed later in this chapter.

The average market price

The average market price for a given product is what most artisans sell similar work for in the same market. In most businesses, this amount is whatever price the market will bear or the most customers will pay. The average market price is also sometimes referred to as the ceiling price.

To find the average market price, survey what is selling where and for how much. This can be an adventure of sorts, going around and scoping out what's happening in the field. However you go about it, you need to make some kind of market survey.

If you plan to sell at craft shows, go around to several and check prices that similar craft items are selling for. Make a list totalling all the different prices you find, then divide this figure by the number of items in the list. This gives you the average price, or the ceiling or, in general, the most you want to ask for your work. If you exceed the ceiling price by much, without using the techniques mentioned in this book about raising perceived value, sales will suffer.

Within the vast marketplace for selling crafts, you can find some markets where one average market price is higher than for similar work in different markets. Prices may even differ dramatically among selling avenues so be aware of the average prices in the specific market you are selling to like home parties, stores, craft fairs, or catalogs.

You can raise the ceiling price by utilizing the techniques we have already mentioned. Increase perceived value through special packaging. Provide extra customer service. Display your work in an elegant booth environment.

It is important to remember that purchasers of arts and crafts are collectors, as well as buyers. If they really want a bargain, they'll go to a garage sale.

If you are paying sales tax on your supplies, register your business with your state tax-ation and revenue division and get a resale sales certificate. A copy of this form should be sent to all your suppliers with a letter from you asking for exemption from paying sales tax on supplies you will be reselling.

Check retail prices for craft items like yours selling in stores and galleries, too. You can assume that the price the store is asking is twice what they actually paid. Your challenge is to know if you can afford to sell your work wholesale and still make a profit. Figuring the floor price, which is explained shortly, will tell you if you can.

You could use the market average as a pricing strategy indefinitely. If you intend to do mostly craft shows, all you need to know is how much the average customer is willing to pay for a given product. Then you need to know whether the price you ask covers all your expenses and allows a profit.

Note that prices will usually differ between a retail store and a craft show for the same item because of the store's higher operating expenses. For example, you may find the average market price for a stain glass work priced at $400 in galleries and the same item priced at $250 at craft shows.

If you are doing a show in a town where you have store accounts, you will want to keep your retail prices the same as what the shop asks. Many store owners shop the fairs for new work. If they see you undercutting their prices, you could easily lose the account.

Determining your cost of goods

Cost of goods is the dollar amount you spend to make or buy products that you resell. This includes all material and labor involved, but not the fixed costs explained later. Cost of goods, when subtracted from your gross sales, leaves an amount known as your gross profit. See Chapter 6, Recordkeeping.

Variable or direct costs

Variable costs include any materials used in constructing your pieces plus the cost of your labor or wages you pay employees to make those items. These are called variable or direct costs because the cost changes with the number of items or kind of items you make.

Material costs

Examples of material costs might include: *For a weaver:* yarn, thread, accessories, dyes. *For a stained glass artist:* glass, solder, lead, finishes, paints. *For a woodworker:* wood, glue, screws, pegs, sandpaper. You would also add in shipping charges, and sales taxes paid.

You can track all your costs per project and refer back to it when you are beginning new projects on a form called a Project Log. See the next page.

When you use small quantities of glues, paints, and so on, it doesn't pay to try and figure these exact amounts. It's more effective to estimate their cost by averaging the use over time.

For example, say you produce fifty dolls the same size over a period of three months. You used three tubes of paint at $3.50 each, two and one half bottles of glue at $4.95 each, three yards of fabric at $4 per yard, 1 yard of ribbon at $8.00 per yard and two yards of lace at $6 per yard.

The bodies and heads of the dolls cost $3.87 each. Following is an example of how to figure your material costs:

50 doll's heads at $3.87 = $193.50

3 tubes paint at $3.50 = $ 10.50

2.5 bottles glue at $4.95 = $ 12.38

3 yards fabric at $4.00 = $ 12.00

1 yard ribbon at $8.00 = $ 8.00

2 yards lace at $6.00 = $ 12.00

total materials = $248.38

$248.38 divided by 50

equal $4.97 for each doll

Total material supplies used for each doll is $4.97. Now double that amount before you add this figure into calculating your final price. Why? Because if a person were to purchase these items themselves, they would pay full retail which is twice what you pay when you buy supplies wholesale.

Additional direct expenses for a project might include any selling commissions you pay to sales reps and advertising done for specific projects.

Chapter 8 gives you many tips for cutting material costs.

Cost of labor

Cost of labor is also a variable cost. It is the dollar value you set for your time in producing your craft and operating your business. It also includes money you pay to employees or contractors for their labor.

The way to get an average cost of your time spent on production is to record your working hours over a one year period. You can then average your time per piece to get a number that approximates your labor costs. You need a realistic average because almost everyone works at a different pace. You may even

Figure 3.1 Project Log example

Project Description:

Photo or sketch:

Materials & Accessories:

Assembly Instructions:

Finishing:

Total Labor Hours and Costs:

Total Cost of Materials:

Total Production Cost:

Retail Price:

Gross Profit:

Notes:

If you need extra help in your business but can't afford to hire full-time employees, you can offer internships to high school students. Depending on how you fulfill some educational require- ments, you can get help for nothing or little cost. For more information, write: The National Society of Experiential Edu- cation, 3509 Haworth Dr #207, Raleigh NC

notice days when you seem to accomplish more than at other times. Record your work time on the Project Log record. Keeping track of the hours you work can also tell you how much time it should take employees to produce a piece if you do hire outside help.

For yourself or employees, the hourly labor rate you come up with as a cost must include an additional thirty percent to cover employment taxes. The thirty percent is an estimate suggested by the Small Business Administration. It includes the average amount you also pay as an employer in Social Security deductions, workers compensation costs, unemployment insurance, bookkeeping, and additional paperwork. If you provide health insurance or a retirement plan for yourself or workers, this amount needs to be accounted for, too.

For instance, you are creating the dolls we just mentioned and you do not hire labor of any kind. You decided that you want to pay yourself $10 per hour. If it takes you two and one half hours to make one doll, figure your cost of labor as:

2.5 times $10 = $25.00

$25 times 30% = $7.50

total labor for one doll = $32.50

Chapter 9 tells you how to reduce labor costs by getting more out of your time and workspace.

Indirect or fixed costs (overhead)

Indirect costs or fixed costs, sometimes called overhead, are those expenses you pay to operate your business on a day to day basis. In general, these expenses remain in a fixed range throughout the year regardless of how much you sell. Examples are licenses, rent, utilities, phone, insurance, advertising, bank charges, office supplies, cleaning supplies, professional dues, and so on.

These expenses are often the most overlooked by crafters who work from home. Possibly this is because it is difficult to mentally associate the price of a physical item one makes with invisible but constant costs of working at home. However, they have to be included in your formula.

Many home based crafters forget to account for business use of the home. Yet there are great tax advantages for a home office and employing family members in the business. For more ways to take advantage of tax breaks for your home business, see Chapter 10.

If you do not include all of the indirect costs in figuring your prices, any financial projection or plan you make about your business will be false and imaginary. Just imagine going out and buying new furniture because you think your business is doing great. Then you do your bookkeeping, after four months of putting it off, and discover you didn't really make the profit you thought you had.

For anyone just starting a business, estimating indirect costs is a challenge. First, you don't really know what it will cost you to do business because there are bound to be expenses you can't imagine. Second, you have only a rough idea, if any, how and when your sales will come. An important solution is to learn to project your cash flow, discussed in detail Chapter 7.

After you've been in business for at least six months, you have enough operating expenses to make a good estimate for the coming year. The following example shows fixed costs for a business over a one year period.

Figure 3.2 Sample list of indirect expenses.

Expenses	Per month	Per year
advertising	$ 20	$ 240
auto	$ 100	$ 1,200
cartons	$ 10	$ 120
freight	$ 20	$ 240
insurance	$ 30	$ 360
bank fees	$ 20	$ 240
laundry	$ 15	$ 180
licenses		$ 40
misc. exp.	$ 30	$ 360
office	$ 10	$ 120
postage	$ 16	$ 192
rent	$ 250	$ 3,000
rent - booths	$ 400	$ 4,800
repairs	$ 10	$ 120
telephone	$ 45	$ 540
publications	$ 10	$ 120
travel	$ 200	$ 2,400
utilities	$ 95	$ 1,140
TOTAL	$1281	$15,412

Total indirect expenses for this example equals $15,412.

Hourly cost of doing business

We want to know the hourly cost of doing business which accounts for all the above costs. Divide $15,412 by the total number of hours worked in one year. For example, if you work 40 hours a week, 48 weeks a year, the total number of hours is 1,920. Divided into the total yearly fixed expenses of $15,412, you get an hourly cost of doing business of $8.03 per hour. This $8.03 does not include the amount of your labor, materials, or desired profit, only what it costs you to operate your business.

I use 'hours you work' as a divider because your labor remains a constant. If you divide your expenses by the total number of pieces you make, the resulting dollar amount does not account for the range of time as labor needed to make different pieces.

The IRS allows deductions of business expenses from your income tax. Tax laws and amounts of what can be deducted change from year to year. Check with your accountant or with the IRS for what deductions can be claimed for the year you are currently figuring expenses.

For example, the use of part of your home for your business may be deductible if you meet IRS requirements for such a claim. Read Chapter 10 in this book.

When you purchase tools or equipment necessary to produce your craft, the cost of the tools may be deductible in total for that year, or if over a specific dollar amount, depreciable over three to five years. Tools, machines, and furniture - like a work table, for example are all assets you will use over time.

The IRS provides free publications outlining guidelines for tax-payers. Call (800) 424-3676 to order Publication 910, GUIDE TO FREE TAX SERVICES. 910 lists publications you may need for a business.

There are IRS guidelines for different types of assets and how they can be depreciated.

Depreciation means you deduct a certain percentage of the cost each year for the following few years. An accountant understands the best use of depreciation for equipment purchases. See Chapter 6 for more on this.

It is important to determine your fixed expenses at least once a year. Rent and utilities go up, you may be spending more on long distance than last year, or you may have purchased newer equipment. To recover these expenses, you must continue to keep account of them and include the most up-to-date figures in your pricing formula.

Profit

Profit is the amount of money you want to make on each piece after paying all the other costs. What are your average living costs? How much does it cost you on a monthly basis to live in the manner to which you are accustomed?

For example, if all your personal living expenses including rent, food, utilities, clothing, automobile, taxes comes to $800 per month or $9,600 per year, that is the amount you need to receive in profits.

Take the total amount of your labor for the year as we did above. If you work 40 hours a week, 48 weeks a year, the total number of hours is 1,920. Divide your living expenses of $9,600 by 1,920 hours and you get $5 per hour. This amount is the profit you wish to make above your labor costs on an hourly basis.

Also, if you put your money in a mutual fund instead of your craft business, you might make 8% to 12% a year in dividends. Why shouldn't you expect to make at least that much profit from your own business?

Figuring the minimum price you must get

While the average market price for your products is the ceiling price or the most you will charge, the formula below will give you the floor price or the lowest price you can safely charge for an item. The floor price insures that you recover your invested expenses and make a fair profit. The floor price accounts for:

- Your cost of goods, that is, the total of your material and labor costs for each item.
- All fixed or indirect costs associated with running your business on a day-today basis. These daily costs are called overhead or fixed expenses because you pay them regularly whether you sell anything or not.
- Profit you want to make.
- Taxes you pay on profits. Taxes are covered more in Chapter 4 and Chapter 10.

The formula for figuring the floor price is:

cost of goods (sum of material + labor costs)

+

indirect costs

+

profit

+

taxes on profit

=

minimum price you must receive

If you sell wholesale, this minimum or floor price will be the lowest amount you can afford to sell to stores for. This doesn't necessarily or always equal what you actually decide to charge. The average market price for similar work may allow you to charge more. But it does mean that if you can't get at least this price, you should not sell wholesale.

Figure the minimum or floor price of every item you make to determine if your current prices are realistic. Chapter 7 tells you how to include the floor price when measuring profitability for each item and each market you sell to.

My first year selling, I priced pieces without including the above expenses. I basically guessed at the amounts I should charge after checking what the average price was for work like mine. When I finally did look at the expenses incurred from all the shows, my labor, and overhead, I found I was producing high quality pieces for about $3 an hour. After learning that, I began upgrading my promotional materials and hang tags. I was then able to raise my prices and increase my hourly return.

Once you know your hourly labor rate, your hourly cost of doing business rate, how much profit you want, and your material costs, you have the basic foundation for determining how much to charge for every new piece you make without reinventing the wheel each time. Also, when you update your records periodically, you will be able to quickly learn if you need to raise prices. Once you know how much to charge for each item you make, you can keep a record of those prices on the Project Log form or a separate sheet that lists all your minimum prices.

The mistake most crafting entrepreneurs make is an error that can turn your dream of financial freedom into a nightmare of endless expenditures. This error is not accounting for all costs involved in producing their craftwork and the costs of getting those products sold.

The next chapter will show you how to discover the not-so-obvious expenses of doing business that often get brushed aside, yet still cost you money and should be accounted for.

> Save on costs of furniture and office equipment by purchasing used office equipment at government auctions. Contact the liquidation officer at your local Small Business Administration or call (800) 827-5722 or your local IRS office and ask for the 24 hour Auction Hotline number.

Chapter 4
Hidden Costs That Steal Profits

"The avoidance of taxes is the only pursuit that still carries any reward."

- John Maynard Keynes

If only we could just forget about taxes, wouldn't life be simpler? Unfortunately, it's one of those ever present costs that will probably not diminish in our lifetimes.

Many self-employed workers overlook taxes as a cost of doing business. Yet taxes and some other less obvious expenses are very real. This chapter will help you recognize hidden costs and how to include them in your pricing considerations.

Income and self-employment taxes

You pay income and self-employment taxes based on income you receive from your business. You should include the cost of taxes in your pricing formula. Say that in your tax bracket, you pay 7% of your net income in combined taxes. To make it simple, add 7% of whatever an item's profit after expenses comes to and add it to the selling price.

For example, if an item's total cost to make including indirect costs is $7 and you sell it for $10, your profit before taxes is $3. You will pay 7% of the $3 or $.21 in income tax. The $7 in costs are deductible expenses from income so you won't pay tax on the $7. To recover the tax the IRS will assess you on the $3 profit, you could add another $.25 to your asking price. Of course, you might also consider whether you can confidently get $10.25 for the item rather than the simpler price of $10. If not, can you lower costs somewhere else?

This section refers to income taxes not sales tax. Sales tax is collected from your customers at the time of the sale and then paid to your state on a regular basis.

Shipping costs

There are usually two types of costs of freight you will need to account for, shipping in and shipping out. You typically pay shipping on materials you purchase by mail. You want to make sure to include this amount in totaling your material costs.

The other typical shipping expense is what you pay to send items to customers through the mail, UPS, or by whatever other means. In most mail order business transactions, customers expect to pay shipping costs. So you bill the customer for shipping and recover this amount when you collect payment. This is the case when selling wholesale to stores or retail to consumers.

Offering free shipping when a customer prepays an order can be a good sales incentive. However, you should know for certain that you can afford to do so or include those shipping costs in your pricing formulas.

What your customers don't expect, and often in fact resent, is a fee sometimes called "packing charge." If you intend to charge extra to cover safe packing for pieces like glass or pottery, include the additional safe packing costs in the item's price.

How to account for sales rep commissions

When you have reached the place in your business where you can produce in quantity and on a predictable schedule, you may want to use sales reps to open more accounts. Commissions paid to reps must then be accounted for in your pricing formula. In general, rep fees amount to between 10% and 30% of the wholesale price.

For example, you sell small toy soldiers for $4 each wholesale. You hire a rep on commission to open new accounts and you agree to the rep's terms of 15% commission on every sale. In this case, that amount is $4 times 15% equals $.60 on each item.

Subtracting $.60 from $4 equals $3.40, the amount you have left after each sale through the rep. Can you afford to sell a toy soldier at $3.40 each? Go to Chapter 7 and follow the steps to determining profitability.

If $3.40 doesn't give you a return of your cost of goods, desired profit, and indirect costs, you will have to raise the wholesale cost to the point where the rep's fees are covered. If the market won't bear raising the price, find ways to reduce those production, labor, and indirect costs.

Professional crafters who develop a large wholesale business eventually ponder the question of whether to use a rep or open new accounts themselves. The issue here involves more than price alone. You have to know how much time you are willing to spend out their selling.

Reps are not usually interested in one-of-a-kind pieces. They want craft items that can be produced in quantity and reordered with confidence. Their market is more likely to be gift stores rather than galleries. Reps expect and will only work with craftpersons who have a reliable production plan. That is, all orders the rep arranges will be filled by the crafter on schedule.

A sales rep will be willing to discuss your wholesale prices with you based on their experience in the market. As long as you know your floor price, you can make a decision whether working with a rep is viable.

For more information on working with wholesale reps, see *Directory of Wholesale Reps for Crafts Professionals* ($15.95) by Sharon Olson. This book is for craftpersons who wish to sell wholesale to gift shops, galleries, museums, department stores, etc.. Olson tells how to select a rep and includes suggestions for beginning craftpersons from the reps themselves.

Cost of sales

The cost of selling your crafts is already included in your fixed or indirect expenses. For example, money spent on booth rental fees comes under "rent." Telephone calls made to store accounts fall under "phone." Even though we have already accounted for the cost of sales under indirect expenses, there are good reasons to look at these costs separately to ascertain whether an item is profitable or not. By determining the cost of sales, you can see which items make more or less money in various markets you sell to. See Chapter 7 for more on profitability.

For instance, you sold jewelry through 23 art and craft shows last year. Also, you spent an average of 30 hours per show, including driving, setup, the hours of the show, tearing down, and driving home. Total hours spent to sell your pieces through these shows for the year were 690. For this example, you have sold a total of 2,000 pieces. Divide 690 hours by the number of items, or 2,000, to get an average time of .35 hours, or approximately twenty minutes selling time per piece.

> # of hours selling = 690
> divided by # of items sold = 2,000
> gives you hours to sell one item = .35

The hourly rate you have decided to pay yourself is $10 an hour and the hourly rate of your fixed costs is $8.03 (see page 43 for figuring hourly fixed costs.)

> hourly labor = $10.00
>
> hourly fixed costs = $8.03
>
> total costs per hour = $18.03
>
> $18.03 per hour times
>
> .35 per hour to make one item
>
> equals cost of sales for one item of $6.31

Suppose you sell your jewelry to stores and you sold 3,000 pieces to shops or galleries in one year. You spent twenty hours a month getting and servicing these accounts. You also spent $575 in producing and mailing catalogs to store owners. Here's how you would figure cost of sales:

> 20 hours x 12 months = 240 hours
>
> 240 hours x $18.03 hourly cost = $4,327.20
>
> producing and mailing catalogs = $575.00
>
> total costs of selling = $4,902.20
>
> $4902.20 divided by 3,000 pieces = $1.64 each

Your cost of sales selling your jewelry to stores in this example is $1.64 per item.

In determining your cost of sales, it doesn't matter so much that you might be selling 20 differently priced items. You probably spend the same amount of time on average selling a $20 set of earrings as you do selling a $100 necklace. What is important is that by looking at cost of sales, you can learn if each item and each market is profitable. For more on this, see Chapter 7.

After learning about all the costs we have talked about in these last two chapters, you may wonder how anyone is able to charge enough to fully recover their expenses while producing craftwork. The fact is many crafters don't recover their costs. They don't stay in business very long either. What you should ask yourself is what is the price you will pay for not getting back the money and time you put into making crafts for a living.

If you want to succeed in a craft or any other kind of business, develop a habit of keeping records of all expenses and sales on a regular basis. If you are working your business part-time, it should only take a couple of hours a month to stay current. If you are a full-time working craftperson, it may take an hour or two every week. Whatever time it takes you, the effort will pay big dividends.

In the past, I often got behind in this particular discipline. Once I went for six months without entering my expenses and sales into my accounting program. After everything was finally entered, I generated reports like those explained in Chapter 7 that showed my income, cost of goods, gross profit, expenses, and profit or loss. I saw instantly that I had made much less profit than I had imagined and quickly began looking for ways to cut my expenses and boost sales.

Chapter 5
Pricing One-of-a-Kind Pieces

*"An artist is a creature driven by
demons. He doesn't know why
they choose him and he's usually
too busy to wonder why."*
                                   - William Faulkner

We all yearn to expand our horizons creatively. Producing an occasional one-of-a-kind piece reminds us of why we got into craft. For many crafters though, it is creating and selling reproducible items that pays the bills.

After my first few seasons as a handweaver, I found I could only do production work for about two months at a stretch before feeling like I was becoming an automaton. Then I would let loose for a week with a new project or design that was truly one-of-a-kind. These break-away pieces took longer to sell but commanded prices three or four times higher than my other production pieces. Still, I was really making these pieces for my own creative satisfaction and to interrupt the routine of production work.

Many crafters may feel that each of their pieces are one-of-a-kind. What this chapter addresses is those works which would fall into the category of art arising from the finest craftsmanship, works which would not be duplicated through production techniques.

Accounting for intrinsic or artistic value

When you create one-of-a-kind works, there are additional pricing considerations to those mentioned in the previous chapters. For instance, how do you account for the intrinsic or artistic value of a piece? How do you value a limited body or series of works? How do you charge for work-for-hire projects?

Pricing by the square foot

Some professional artists and fine crafters like to quote on commissioned work at a set rate by the square foot. This amount is determined by their experience doing previous commissions and varies with their assessment of the current project.

For instance, a fiber artist creating large tapestry pieces might charge $100 per square foot or more. This artist knows her labor, studio expenses, materials costs and very close to how long it will take to complete the new piece. A stained glass artist might also charge $120 per square foot based on a different set of costs such as amount of glass and other materials and supportive construction required.

These amounts are arrived at by using the same formulas already discussed. You add your indirect costs and desired profit to come up

If you work from home like most craft artists, here's a handy tip for saving time recording your business calls from your personal phone bill. Your long distance service provider may be able to give you 'account codes' for your calls. After this service is turned on, when you dial long distance, you hear a tone then enter a code. Assign different codes for family members and for business calls. The long distance service provides a breakdown on your monthly bill. Inquire with your provider.

with an hourly cost of doing business. Then add the labor, hourly cost of doing business, desired profit, and taxes on the profit.

When you do commission work, you may want to break down your labor into categories for the sake of billing purposes. For instance, you spend so many hours designing a project, so much time laying out the pieces, more time installing and additional hours adding the finishing touches. This will help you in future estimations.

Working with galleries

Many one-of-a-kind pieces are sold through a gallery or broker. The agent or dealer can help determine a piece's price because of their experience in art sales.

The challenge for the new artisan is that dealers are mainly concerned with getting sales. Because a major consideration in pricing art or high-end craft art is the reputation of the artist, the newer artisan's work may be seen as low end merchandise.

The longer you are in the business of selling one-of-a-kind pieces, the easier it will be to price your work at its market value in galleries.

A way to get started is to shop galleries for pieces similar to yours. Ask the gallery manager for a resume of any craft artisans who show work like what you do. By comparing the background of artists producing work like yours, you can estimate what you should be charging based on your resume. Remember that the gallery is adding a markup to all work shown, probably around 100%.

When presenting your work to a gallery or dealer, have a price sheet with suggested retail prices. In this way you account for dealer markup, usually 100% of the wholesale amount, and there will be no later confusion as to how much you will actually receive from the dealer. For instance, say you've created a sculpture for which you must receive $500. Your price sheet will show a suggested retail price of $1,000.

How to account for broker's fees

If you are working through a broker, agent, or sales rep, the commission you pay them should be added to the total price when you first make a bid or quotation on a job.

There is a simple formula for adding the agent's percentage that leaves you the required amount. Say that you want $4,000 for a piece and the agent will receive 33% as commission. You need to find the total amount that subtracting 33% from that will leave you with $4,000.

Divide the $4,000 by the percentage going to you (100% - 33% = 67%, or .67). $4,000 divided by .67 = $5,970. To check it, simply subtract 33% (.33) of $5,970. This gives you $1,970 for the agent and $4,000 for you.

Make sure you have also added in time you spent creating any models or samples, meetings with the designers, delivery, and installation costs. By the way, you should receive half of any fees in advance to purchase materials needed. Ask for the balance of payment to be due on completion and installation.

An excellent way to successfully market one-of-a-kind pieces is to maintain a customer mailing list and mail postcards when you create new pieces or exhibit in the customer's area. Many collectors are absolutely obsessed with owning a series of pieces by their favorite artists.

How to price commission work

After you have put your name and reputation in the marketplace to such an extent that brokers, interior designers, and architects know who you are, where you are and what you do, you start to receive more opportunities to bid on commissioned work. These purchasers invest in an artist's future success and reputation, as much as the work they buy today.

Success in the interiors and corporate marketplace revolves around professionalism. Part of that professional image is giving a confident presentation of what you can do. Corporate buyers look for and expect consistent price quotes.

Before you can quote accurately on a commission, you need to thoroughly understand Chapter 3, *The Minimum Price to Ask,* Chapter 4, *Hidden Costs,* and Chapter 6, *Recordkeeping.*

Suppose you're commissioned to do a new piece that is not a purchase of an existing work. How do you quote on the job? Here are elements you must include:

- How closely can you estimate your labor required? Remember, there is almost always a deadline for completion of commissioned work. Don't hesitate to increase your first estimate. If something can go wrong, it will.
- Will the materials require special treatment which could increase the cost? Examples include flame retarding, preserving the colors of any materials affected by light, and maintenance costs through the years.
- Are there fees payable to a broker, agent, or subcontractor? Are there extra costs for installation?
- Does your agreement include a provision for unseen problems that were not apparent when you first made a quote on the job? You should add such a paragraph that protects you from hidden costs like structural supports, reinforcement parts, labor and equipment, extra travel time and expenses should you have to return to the installation site afterward.

Unusual circumstances

If you create custom work on commission, you should have an agreement which includes a formula or percentage to add to your quoted price which allows for customers who change their mind. That is, people who switch choices on a color or material after you have quoted on a project. Also, there may be times when you might have to substitute materials because you can no longer get a particular ingredient.

You should also include a clause in your agreements allowing a percentage of increase should specified materials be unavailable due to factors you cannot control. If you don't have such an agreement, you could lose money.

One easy way of handling special orders which may create extra time or trouble is to simply quote a price 5% to 10% higher than normal.

Now you have an idea of all the costs involved in producing and selling craftwork professionally. How do you keep track of all the important data that eventually allows you to arrive at an intelligent price? Perhaps one of the most important aspects of being in business is good recordkeeping.

Do you know how to write a business plan? A great way to start is by ordering THE BUSINESS PLAN FOR HOME-BASED BUSINESS ($1). It provides a solid approach to help you make a business plan. Order from: SBA Publications, P.O. Box 30, Denver CO 80201.

59

Chapter 6
Recordkeeping, A Needed Discipline

*"Some people regard discipline
as a chore. For me it is a kind of
order that sets me free to fly."*
- Julie Andrews

There is one aspect of being self-employed which seems to be universally dreaded, recordkeeping. Perhaps this is because it reminds us of homework assignments we were given in school.

Keeping up with your business records is like homework. Only the grade may be more important now than it was then. The grade is whether you have enough money to pay your bills and feed your family.

Getting to the right price is important. If you do your bookkeeping homework and follow the guidelines in this book, you can be confident you will arrive at the right prices. The key activity is to record and analyze your expenses and sales on a regular basis.

When to start keeping records

You should start keeping records from the day you start planning to do business. Begin by gathering all business related receipts and writing them down in a general accounting journal purchased at an office supply store or on forms like those found in this chapter.

The important point is to have a system you can follow up with regular entries. You can then extract meaningful reports from the information. Since Uncle Sam requires accurate records, you are legally responsible to do so.

Hiring an accountant

Should you hire an accountant or C.P.A.? For most self-employed, the expense of hiring an in-house bookkeeper or accountant can only be justified when the business becomes so large that the owner can't handle it alone anymore. Whether you hire an accountant or not, you should know basic bookkeeping skills. You don't have to have a degree or even formal training to learn accounting.

We highly recommend *Small Time Operator, How to Start Your Own Business, Keep Your Books, Pay Taxes & Stay Out of Trouble!* ($16.95) by Bernard Kamoroff, C.P.A.. This is a complete guide for anyone starting a small business. Covers everything including permits and licenses, insurance, financing, leases, business plans, bookkeeping, taxes, employees, partnerships, corporations, trademarks, dealing with the IRS, and much more. To order, call 1-800-235-6570.

You can also take a basic accounting class from your local community college or continuing education program. Small Business Development Centers or SBDC's sometimes offer courses and many provide free counseling. For an office near you, contact the lead SBDC's listed in the appendix.

Whether you do your own bookkeeping or hire some else, when it's tax time, you will come out ahead by paying an accountant for end of the year tax filings. They are more aware of legitimate deductions you may be missing as well as up to date on changes in the tax laws.

What kind of records to keep track of

There are several basic kinds of records you to keep up with. Here are the ones you are most likely to need followed by samples. You will find blank forms for most in the appendix:

- Business Checkbook
- General Accounting Ledger
- Inventory Log
- Fixed Assets or Depreciation
- Accounts Receivable
- Accounts Payable
- Payroll Log
- Telephone Log
- Mileage, Travel & Entertainment Log
- Weekly Income/Sales Journal

If you haven't already opened a separate checking account for your business, you should do so. You can easily confuse business and personal transactions if they are both present in your personal checking account. When tax time rolls around, you'll be grateful you kept your business records separate.

Depreciation of assets

Some of your assets that were purchased for business use are expenses that will be deducted over time. This is called depreciation. A portion of the cost of the assets is deductible over several years until the entire costs are accounted for. These assets are called fixed assets.

There are different types of assets and the IRS assigns different periods for their depreciation. The tax laws for depreciation change frequently. If you have large expenditures on fixed assets, the safe path to follow is to use a C.P.A.. Here is what you need to give to the expert:

- Date purchased or brought into use.
- Description of equipment or asset.
- Method of depreciation - see your accountant.
- Depreciation schedule - the number of years over which the asset is being written off.
- How much of the asset such as a vehicle is used for business or personal.
- Cost of the asset.

Keeping records by hand

Keeping records can be done by hand on paper or by entering information into a computer. If you are just beginning your business and have no experience with personal computers, you may find it simpler to keep records on paper. An excellent general recordkeeping journal is *Dome's Simplified Weekly Bookkeeping Record* by Nicholas Picchione, C.P.A. (at office supply stores.) You may also want a plastic filing box or metal filing cabinet to separate and store all your records. For example, one divider will say "Rent" and contain rental receipts. Another divider might read "Cost of Materials" and include records of your purchases.

Figure 6.1 Business Checkbook

CHECKING ACCT. REGISTER

DATE	CHECK #	PAYEE	PAID	DEPOSIT	BALANCE
					$1,409.77
2/30/97	1003	Pacific Bell - phone	$45.68		
3/1/97		United Bank		$654.00	
3/1/97	1004	Mr. Meyer - rent	$400.00		$1,618.09

Figure 6.2 Inventory Log

INVENTORY: RAG RUGS

DATE	SOLD TO:	UNITS MADE	UNITS SOLD	BALANCE ON HAND
				23
4/5/97		4		27
4/6/97	Tree Store		6	21
4/11/97		14		35
4/17/97	Arthur Lee Gifts		20	15

As you enter your sales and finished products regularly, you will always know how much to make of each item. You can also learn when to drop items that haven't been selling. You will need an inventory of finished goods every year for your business income tax filing.

Figure 6.3 Accounts Receivable

ACCOUNTS RECEIVABLE

DATE	INVOICE #	CUSTOMER	DUE DATE	AMT. CHARGE	AMT. PAID
10/23/97	101	Village Crafts	11/22/97	$653.42	
10/25/97	97	Linda's Gifts	10/20/97		$213.44
11/1/97	95	Rita Mays	11/2/97		$52.33
				ENDING BALANCE	$387.65

Accounts Receivable means money owed to you by people or businesses you have extended credit to. In the above example, the ending balance $387.65 is the total amount owed to the business. In accounting terms, Accounts Receivables are accounted for as 'Assets.'

Figure 6.4 Accounts Payable

ACCOUNTS PAYABLE

DATE	INVOICE #	VENDOR	DUE DATE	AMT. CHARGE	AMT. PAID
4/3/97	C9876	Flower Supplies	5/2/97	$332.11	
5/1/97	8888	Max Office	6/1/97	$54.98	
5/3/97	C9876	Flower Supplies	5/2/97		$332.11
				ENDING BALANCE	$54.98

Accounts Payable means money you owe for goods and services used in the business. In the above example, the ending balance $54.98 represents the total you owe. This is accounted for under 'Liabilities.'

Figure 6.5 Payroll Log

WEEKLY PAYROLL RECORD						
		DEDUCTIONS				
EMPLOYEE	TOTAL WAGES	SOC. SEC.	MED.	FED. INC. TAX	OTHER	PAID
Mary Gray	$214.00	$14.98		$17.12		$181.90

With a payroll log, you can track hourly wages and witholding taxes for any employees.

Figure 6.6 Telephone Log

TELEPHONE LOG				
2/13	10:00 am	303-123-4567 Brown Gallery	5 min.	$4.38
2/14	8:30 am	503-144-3232 Office Max	5 min	$0.35
2/14	9:15 am	450-333-7787 Tree Gallery	12 min.	$3.99
2/15	5:10 pm	906-656-4321 landlord	4 min.	$2.56

If you operate your business from your home and the phone is your name, not your business name, you will need to keep a log of all your business related calls. Record the date, time, party, length, and reason for the call.

Figure 6.7 Mileage Log

MILEAGE LOG				
DATE	BEGINNING MILEAGE	ENDING MILEAGE	TOTAL MILES DRIVEN	REASON FOR TRIP
8/5/97	45670	45699	29	PICK UP SHELVES
8/7/97	45699	45809	110	PHOENIX SHOW
8/9/97	45809	45812	3	POST OFFICE

There are two ways to deduct your auto expenses. One is by depreciating the car yearly and accounting for all the gas, oil, tires and repairs. A much simpler way is to record all the miles driven for buisness purposes.

Figure 6.7 Travel Expenses

TRAVEL & ENTERTAINMENT LOG				
DATE	LOCATION	REASON	CLIENT	COST
3/15/97	Olive Tree Rest. Denver	dinner to discuss new products	Betty Sue buyer - Blooms	$49.50
4/7/97	Applebee's - Phoenix	eat out while travel	in town for show	$11.34
4/7/97	Motel 8 - Phoenix	lodging while travel	show	$35.95

Many craftpersons travel to sell their work. Use a log like the above to account for your lodging and eating out expenses.

Figure 6.9 Weekly Income Record

WEEKLY INCOME RECORD		
DAY	**TOTAL RECEIPTS FROM BUSINESS**	**AMOUNT**
SUN		
MON	payment from Village Crafts	$437.67
TUES		
WED	class for community college	$35.00
THUR		
FRI	show in Las Vegas	$407.90
SAT	show in Las Vegas	$1,304.56
TOTAL THIS WEEK		$2,185.13
TOTAL UP TO THIS WEEK		$6,755.87
TOTAL TO DATE		$8,941.00

If you don't use a bookkeeping journal, you can track your income on a form like Figure 6.9. It gives you a running total of your income by the week and up to date.

Keeping records by computer

A paper recordkeeping system will work well until you reach a point when increased sales take too much time to record entries by hand. At this point, using a computer will become more cost effective. You will know that time is near when you find yourself spending more time than you can afford to spend looking up records, writing invoices, or trying to do a cash flow projection or balance report on the financial state of your company. Another signal will be when you want to mail new product information or announcement of a special sale to 200 customers and you have to copy their names and addresses by hand.

There are many computer software programs to help small business owners manage their records. Most are sophisticated enough to give you in-depth reports on all aspects of your business in seconds. *QuickBooks* by Intuit is recommended by the Small Business Administration and the program used by this author. *QuickBooks* is very easy to setup and customize to your particular business needs. This program also allows you to generate many kinds of reports quickly and track sales by item or any other kind of classification such as color or size. *QuickBooks* will also let you enter a customer's name, address, and other information and fills

Figure 6.10 Depreciation of Asset

DEPRECIATION	
Date purchased or first used	7/1/95
Description	1994 Toyota Van
Method of depreciation	
Depreciation schedule	5 years
Percent used for business	$0.90
Cost	$11,000.00
Balance to be depreciated	$11,000.00
Depreciated 1995	$3,060.00
Balance to be depreciated	$7,940.00
Depreciated 1996	$4,900.00
Balance to be depreciated	$3,040.00
Depreciated 1997	$2,950.00
Balance to be depreciated	$90.00
Depreciated 1998	$90.00
Balance to be depreciated	
Depreciated 1999	
Balance to be depreciated	
Depreciated 2000	

it in for you automatically when you begin typing the first few letters, which saves time when producing an invoice or statement.

Among the many other computerized accounting packages are *M.Y.O.B. (Mind Your Own Business)* and *Peachtree Accounting.*

The Crafts Report has

Discount office supplies can be bought by mail. Save money and time by shopping at home through a catalog. Call:
Quill (800)789-1331
OfficeMax(800)788-8080
Wholesale Supply Co.
(800)962-9162

regular features on using a computer in your craft business. They also review software programs designed for professional crafters. If you are considering working with such a program, it would be worth the time it takes to read a review or get the opinion of an experienced crafting computer user. *The Crafts Report* is a highly recommended, monthly magazine covering many topics for professional crafters. Subscribe for around $30 a year by calling 800-777-7098.

See the appendix for blank forms mentioned in this chapter and throughout the book. You can photocopy and enlarge them for your own use.

Chapter 7
Are You Making a Profit?

> *"The trouble with the profit system has always been that it was highly unprofitable to most people."*
>
> - E. B. White

Once you have a recordkeeping system in place, you can effectively analyze your sales and expenses to see where there are strengths and weaknesses in the way you do business. Without this knowledge, you might be selling thousands of pieces and still not be profitable. This chapter shows you how to create financial statements to keep you informed and up-to-date.

Financial reports will tell you your break-even point. They will give you a clear picture of your business's financial health. They will also tell you whether each of the products you make is profitable. Learn to use these reports regularly and you will see exactly where action or changes is needed at any given moment. You'll also be able to chart a secure course for the future.

All of the reports mentioned in this chapter are based on your having gathered the data from your records discussed in the last chapter. If you are just starting your business and don't have existing records to use, you'll have to guess about sales and expenses. After about six months to a year, you'll have a better estimate of the numbers.

Are you breaking even?

Break-even is when your total costs or expenses equal your sales or income. The formula is:

selling price x number of units sold = net sales

For instance, say you are a stained glass artist and your average piece sells to stores for $50 and your expenses average $900 per month. Here is how you would determine the number of items you would have to sell to meet your expenses given those figures. "Y" is the number of units you need to sell.

$$\$50 \times Y = \$900$$
$$\$50Y = \$900$$
$$Y = \$900 / \$50$$
$$Y = 18$$

You must sell 18 pieces a month to meet your costs of staying in business. That, however, does not tell you if the piece you are selling at $50 is priced profitably.

Item profitability

Profitability is especially critical when deciding whether to sell to stores, catalogs, or through a sales rep. Unless you know exactly what your costs are, you could quote a price and make an agreement with a wholesale buyer or sales rep where you end up losing money. The following chart shows exactly how much profit you make on an item. Create a chart for every product you make.

Figure 7.1 Profit Table

PROFIT FOR: Bird House (large)				
MARKET	Price	Production Cost	Cost of Sales	Profit
CRAFT SHOWS	$35.00	$12.00	$15.00	$8.00
HOME SHOWS	$35.00	$12.00	$2.00	$11.00
INTERIOR DESIGNERS	$22.00	$12.00	$7.00	$3.00
REPS TO STORES	$22.50	$12.00	$16.00	($4.50)
CATALOGS	$24.50	$12.00	$12.00	$0.50

In the above table, production cost is the sum of materials, labor, and indirect costs that we looked at in Chapter 3.

The next step in using such information is to take the number of units sold for each market over a given period and multiply this times the amount of profit. That will give you a more complete picture of where your strongest markets and profits are coming from. Likewise, it will tell you what markets to pull out of.

For example, look at the following table for the number of bird houses sold.

In Figure 7.2, there is more volume of profit from selling at craft shows than any other market, even though sales at home shows were more profitable per sale. Another element to consider is the ease of sales. Catalog sales, for instance, only require one sale, i.e. to the catalog buyer. The catalog company handles all fulfillment and collections.

In Figure 7.2, it might pay to see if the retail price of the large bird house could be raised to $40 from $35 without loss of sales.

Figure 7.2 Profit/Volume Table

YEAR's PROFIT/VOLUME FOR: Bird House (large)			
MARKET	Units Sold	Profit	Total Volume
CRAFT SHOWS	133	$8.00	$1,064.00
HOME SHOWS	21	$11.00	$231.00
INTERIOR DESIGNERS	3	$3.00	$9.00
REPS TO STORES	50	($4.50)	($225.00)
CATALOGS	670	$0.50	$335.00

Such an increase would bring an extra $665 profit at the end of the year.

By looking at each market you sell to, you can see right away which products are making or losing money and then make a decision about what actions to take. In the above example, selling the large bird house is seen to be actually losing money through rep sales. Therefore, you would look at whether any costs could be reduced or consider canceling sales through reps.

You have control over your prices. Recordkeeping helps you learn the exact cost you must recover. You may be able to lower your prices in certain circumstances. For instance, you find yourself faced with many competing crafts similar to yours. Lowering your prices may make the difference to customers faced with similar products. By lowering your asking price, you will also lower your gross profit. But you might actually increase net profits because of higher volume.

Financial reports

Financial reports and statements are put together from the information you have recorded on the record forms mentioned before.

Financial reports are used:

*   In determining a correct price for all your products.
*   When figuring your taxes.
*   In writing a business plan.
*   When applying for a loan.
*   When you need to know the status of your business.
*   When identifying strengths and weaknesses.
*   When preparing to sell a business.
*   When taking on investors' capital.

If you make frequent use of financial reports to see how your business is doing, you will succeed over those who only pay attention to their products and sales. Your accounting reports are a lot like x-rays of internal organs. And like a doctor, you examine these x-rays to see how the patient, your business, is doing.

There are three financial statements that are vitally important to have available on short notice. These are known as "Cash Flow Projection," "Balance Sheet," and "Profit or Loss Statement."

Cash Flow Projection

The Cash Flow Projection is a forecast of how money comes into and flows out of your business. You use it as a projected budget to tell you when you are most likely to need more cash for operating expenses.

Money comes in from sales of your craftwork, teaching classes, selling excess materials, loans, and whatever additional income streams your business creates. This money is used to run

Figure 7.3 Cash Out List

CASH OUT (for next year)	
START UP COSTS	
business permits/licenses	$40.00
other	
DIRECT COSTS	
labor	$1,960.00
materials	$3,975.00
freight	$567.00
miscellaneous	$2,109.00
TOTAL DIRECT COSTS	$8,651.00
INDIRECT EXPENSES	
rent	$3,600.00
utilities	$1,500.00
insurance	$1,800.00
phone	$600.00
travel	$2,400.00
TOTAL INDIRECT COSTS	$9,900.00
ASSETS	
long term purchases	$2,400.00
DEBTS OR LIABILITIES	
loan payments	$3,600.00
OWNER'S SALARY	$24,000.00
TOTAL CASH OUT	$48,551.00

the business, pay off loans and interest, and for your personal salary. For instance, if you need $25,000 a year to operate the business plus a salary for yourself of $25,000, you will need to generate $50,000 of total income just to stay even.

The benefit of the Cash Flow Projection is that you can estimate how much you money you will have and *when you will need it.* A business can be profitable and still fail because of lack of cash on hand when bills are due.

For instance, what happens frequently in a craft business is you take the money you have on hand and invest it in materials or show rental fees, usually months in advance of actual show dates. Now you no longer have that money to pay for more immediate expenses like rent or phone. The endless catch-22 is that you must continue to invest in materials and reserve selling places in order to carry on the activities that will bring in income.

The Cash Flow Projection helps you plan ahead for sources of cash to allow you to keep operating until sales are coming in. You can build a simple Cash Flow Projection by first listing all the cash flowing out of your business and all the cash flowing in for a

Figure 7.4 Cash In List

CASH IN (for next year)	
BEGINNING CASH ON HAND	$3,444.00
SALES-INCOME	
craft shows	$28,655.00
stores	$13,098.00
catalogs	$4,012.00
teaching	$1,345.00
OTHER INCOME	
interest	$12.00
SALES OF ASSETS	$200.00
LOANS	
PERSONAL INVESTMENT	
TOTAL CASH IN	$50,766.00

specific period, usually the coming year. A Cash Out List would include:

• Start-up costs to get your business going like licenses, permits, and stationery.
• Direct expenses like labor and material costs to produce an inventory of goods to sell.
• Indirect expenses like rent, utilities, phone, etc.
• Assets or long-term purchases like equipment, building, or vehicle.
• Debts or liabilities, that is payments on loans.
• Your salary.
   A Cash In List would include:
• Beginning cash on hand in cash or bank accounts.
• Income from sales, teaching, selling supplies, payments to accounts receivables, and deposits on orders.
• Other income like interest or dividends.
• Sale of assets like property, equipment, buildings, or vehicles.
• Loans from banks, credit unions, friends, or credit cards.
• Personal investment, that is, putting in money from your personal assets to keep the business going.

With the two lists of Cash In and Cash Out for the coming year, you can put together a working Cash Flow Projection sometimes also called a Pro-Forma Income Statement. You will then know where your money will come from and how much you will need to pay out. You will also need to know when all of this is going to take place. If you use a computer accounting program like *QuickBooks,* this is one of many reports that can be generated automatically *and very quickly.* The program adds all the previous records you specify and then projects the trends of cash out and cash in forward for the period you choose.

If you are doing accounting by hand, the table following will give you a starting place. The importance of a monthly and yearly Cash Flow Projection cannot be underestimated. Using your previous year's records and a little guesswork, you can project forward for the coming twelve months to learn when you will experience a cash crunch or a possible cash surplus.

You can also use the Cash Flow Projection to create a picture of how lowering or rasing your prices will affect your cash on hand and end of the year profits. For instance, if you are thinking of raising a product's price from $10 to $12, multiply the number of units you sold last year times $2. Then make a new Cash Flow Statement, this time adding the number of units sold times the increase in price to your income line. Now you can see how raising the price will affect your cash on hand.

If after completing a Cash Flow Projection you anticipate future cash flow problems, here are some ways of improving Cash In:

• Do more craft fairs and home parties where cash comes to you direct from sales.

• Do less wholesale business where stores often take 30, 60, or 90 days to pay.

• Require at least 50% down on special orders with balance due in thirty days.

• Accept credit cards. When deposited to your account, you get immediate credit and use of funds.

• Buy supplies and services on thirty days terms. Make this an immediate goal whenever engaging a new service or purchasing from a new supplier.

• Sell what you got first, worry about producing later.

Figure 7.5 Cash Flow Statement

CASH FLOW for: Month of September			
	IN-FLOW	OUT-FLOW	BALANCE
BEG. CASH BALANCE 9/1			$2,300.00
Sept. 1 thru Sept. 7			
rent due		$300.00	
ads		$175.00	
freight		$23.00	$1,802.00
sales thru 9/7	$350.00		$1,452.00
weekly to date total	$350.00	$498.00	
Sept. 8 thru Sept. 15			
materials purchase		$532.00	
office supplies		$18.00	
sales thru 9/15	$209.00		$1,111.00
weekly to date total	$559.00	$1,048.00	
Sept. 16 thru Sept. 23			
insurance		$123.00	
car payment		$237.00	
utilities		$87.00	
sales thru 9/23	$24.00		$688.00
weekly to date total	$583.00	$1,495.00	
Sept. 24 thru Sept. 30			
cash - personal		$100.00	
show deposit		$450.00	
material purchase		$81.00	
sales thru 9/30	$657.00		$714.00
weekly to date total	$1,240.00	$2,126.00	
CASH ON HAND 9/30			$714.00

Figure 7.6 Balance Sheet

BALANCE SHEET as of November 25	
ASSETS	
Current Assets	
Checking/Savings Accounts	$2,356.44
Accounts Receivable	$896.43
Inventory Assets	$7,433.21
Consigned Inventory Assets	$709.00
Fixed Assets	
Land	
Buildings	
Equipment	$2,134.54
Furniture	$478.65
Vehicles	$3,522.00
Other Assets	
Total Current Assets	$17,530.27
LIABILITIES	
Current Liabilities	
Accounts Payable	$456.77
Notes Payable, due within one year	$240.50
TAXES PAYABLE	
Federal Income Tax	$237.89
State Income Tax	$22.45
Self Employment Tax	$18.71
Sales Tax	$23.21
Long Term Liabilities	$3,077.89
Total Liabilities	$4,077.42
OWNER'S EQUITY	$13,452.85
	$17,530.27

- Run periodical specials to reduce slow moving and closeout inventory.

- Avoid using your personal credit cards to finance your business unless you commit to paying the bill in thirty days. What may appear as a quick fix to a cash flow problem can quickly become an unconscious habit of putting off payments. Soon interest rates are accumulating and cash for other expenses has to go toward credit card bills.

Balance Sheet

A Balance Sheet is a report showing the status of your business as of the date of the statement. It shows the viewer or a prospective lender whether you are in a healthy or weak position. As you can see in Figure 7.6, a Balance Sheet shows your assets, liabilities, and net worth. Assets are what you own of value like equipment, property, vehicles, and inventory. Liabilities are debts owed by you to lenders such as business loans, mortgages (on business property), credit cards used for the business, or personal loans for your business made by friends. Net worth is the amount of your equity or owner investment. Equity is an amount equal to your assets minus your liabilities.

Slash your long distance bills. Get low interstate rate of 3.9 cents per minute, 24 hours a day, billed in 6 second increments. No sign-up fee. This service is unlike most other carriers like ATT, MCI, and Sprint, who all bill you in 1 min. increments so you pay for time you don't use. To enroll, see www.maktrix.com.

Profit and Loss Statement

A Profit and Loss Statement shows specific business activities

Figure 7.7 Profit and Loss Statement

PROFIT & LOSS INCOME STATEMENT			
INCOME			
	Catalog Sales	$3,567.00	
	Craft Show Sales	$24,762.00	
	Store Sales	$1,705.00	
	Home Party Sales	$5,409.00	
	TOTAL INCOME		$35,443.00
	Cost of Goods Sold		($8,777.00)
	GROSS PROFIT		$26,666.00
EXPENSES			
	Ads	$1,525.00	
	Auto	$2,768.70	
	Bank charges	$195.67	
	Equipment	$365.86	
	Freight	$567.80	
	Interest	$41.02	
	Miscellaneous	$325.61	
	Office supplies	$234.17	
	Publications	$55.66	
	Phone	$953.55	
	Rent	$3,524.00	
	Travel	$987.50	
	Utilities	$1,349.94	
	TOTAL EXPENSES		$12,894.48
NET INCOME (before taxes)			$13,771.52

over a given period. It is also called an Income Statement because it shows where your income is coming from and how you spent money for that time period. This report lets you see areas of greatest expense and which of your sales activities generate the most income. Much of the information used in generating the Cash Flow Statement will be used for generating a Profit and Loss Statement. Profit and Loss tells you where you've been while Cash Flow tells you where you're headed.

For instance in Figure 7.7, you can see how expenses compare to income. Were all these costs completely necessary? Could travel or other expenses be reduced?

Financial reports allow you to make informed decisions about what to do to increase profits or reduce expenses. If your sales are over $2,000 a month, you should probably generate the Profit and Loss Statement at least once every three months to learn where you stand.

Simple, clear business analysis is needed if you want to survive in business. It is a matter of creating the statements we have shown in this chapter based on all your records or projections. Once you have started a recordkeeping system, all you have to do is plug in new numbers every four months or so to get a complete overview of your business.

Take the time to sit down and do this periodically. You will then be working in reality, not imagination. Do this and your business will prosper. Neglect recordkeeping and you might want to start looking for your next employer.

Chapter 8
How To Cut Material Costs

*"I did not have three thousand
pairs of shoes, I had one
thousand and sixty."*
                    - Imelda Marcos

The longer you are in business, the more knowledge you gain about your craft and its industry. Though you may think your expenses and costs are pretty well fixed, experience will bring insights over time that allow you to find more and more ways to save money. This chapter will give you a jump start on where you can begin saving today.

Working with wholesale suppliers

At some point in buying supplies, you will realize greater savings by buying in bulk. Some craft supply wholesalers will sell to professional crafters, some will not. You will be treated by suppliers according to how you present your company to them from the first approach.

To better your chances of getting an account, contact them as if you owned a retail store. Many wholesalers will be satisfied with seeing your business stationery, business cards, a separate checking account and letter of credit acceptance from other major suppliers. However, some might ask for photos of your 'store front.'

Wholesale suppliers give the best discounts to retail dealers. Though many suppliers will give discounts to professional crafters, the discounts are often less than to a store.

Don't be discouraged if a big supplier turns you down. Just keep trying until you've managed to open accounts with any suppliers who will give you thirty days terms (net 30) to pay your bills. As with credit cards, the more credit you get, the more you will receive.

If your business alone does not generate enough sales to justify buying supplies in large quantities, join together with friends or friendly competitors in a similar position to make a big purchase. See if fellow crafters or guild members can help make up the remainder of the order. Networking this way helps everyone.

Sources of wholesale supplies

There are several means of locating craft supply companies who might sell products direct to you. Companies who advertise in magazines related to your craft are a good place to start though you may not get the true wholesale price unless you are a store. Art and craft show guide magazines also carry ads by wholesalers. See *The Crafts Report* and *ProCrafter Magazine.*

You can also get discounts on purchases through membership in the National Crafts Association founded in 1983. They publish directories of wholesale craft sources and many additional directories like wholesale craft reps and stores and galleries that buy crafts. NCA serves members as a clearinghouse for marketing and business help. For more information, contact National Crafter's Association, 2012 Ridge Rd. East, Rochester, NY 14622, 1-800-715-9594, www.craftassoc.com.

You can also find suppliers and meet their representatives in person by attending one of the wholesale craft supply trade shows put on by the Association for Creative Craft Industries (ACCI). To learn more about upcoming events, contact ACCI, Offinger Management, Box 2188, Zanesville, OH 43702 or call (614) 452-4541.

Turn your supply needs into a second income

I turned my wholesale supply buying into a mail order retail supply business, complete with business stationery, tax identification and reseller number, and separate checking account to appear as a legitimate retail outlet. This opened many doors for me with wholesalers. I was also able, in some cases, to buy directly from factories who would have otherwise not sold to me.

There is another reason for going the route of becoming a retail supplier. You can make a profit on excess inventory by selling these supplies to beginning crafters or other customers. Some crafters have found so much business coming their way, they have opted for running the supply business full-time.

After a few initial prepaid purchases, most suppliers will grant you thirty days terms to pay otherwise known as 'ordering on account' or 'net 30.' This helps

If you have large credit card debt, you can get counseling through an agency like Consumer Credit Counseling. Check your Yellow Pages under "Credit Counseling & Debt." They can help you renegotiate your credit card interest rates and consolidate your bills into one payment. Be wary of credit counseling services which charge big fees. For more information, call Family Service America (800) 221-2681, or Christian Financial Concepts (800) 722-1976.

you because you have an extra month's use of cash from sales before paying for supplies.

How much materials to have on hand

A problem for the beginning professional crafter is that they are often cash strapped and can only afford to spend enough to produce items they feel certain they can sell reasonably soon. Almost every new business owner faces the dilemma of how much of their precious cash to spend on materials and inventory and how much to reserve for marketing. I found in the first couple of years selling my handwoven and fiber art, I put much of the profit back in yarns to work with. In fact, I put back too much. I soon found I had an increasing stock of raw materials which I had neglected to relate to future production needs.

One solution is to start with enough raw materials to produce the number of finished pieces you think you will sell in the first six months.

Thereafter, every time you sell a piece from your inventory of finished goods, put aside the amount of material costs - you get this from your records - in a separate checking account just for purchases of supplies. This method allows you to recover your investment in supplies and not get seduced into buying more materials than you are selling. If you don't do this, you may end up supporting a consumer habit rather than running a business.

Many crafters make use of scraps and leftover materials for constructing smaller pieces. By maximizing your materials in this way, you can achieve a lower unit cost. For instance, a weaver might produce several yards of fabric used to construct garments. The cutouts not used for the garments could be used to make handbags, earrings, belts, scarves, and so on. A woodworker who makes furniture or other big projects can use scraps for constructing wooden gift boxes or toys.

Nature is a generous supplier

Some crafters incorporate materials found freely in nature. The only cost is the labor and time involved.

Two more elements involved in improving your profitability are working hours and working space. Experience over time will teach you numerous shortcuts. The next two chapters give you a head start on how to become your business's own efficiency expert.

Credit problems from a divorce? WOMEN & CREDIT HISTORIES is a free booklet telling how to get credit in your own name and what to do if you are denied credit. Write to: Public Reference Branch, Federal Trade Commission, 6th & Pennsylvaina Ave NW, Washington DC 20580 (202) 326-2222.

Chapter 9
Getting More Profit From Your Time & Workspace

*"Have a place for
everything and keep the
thing somewhere else.
This is not advice, it is
merely custom."*
    - Mark Twain

The bottom line for any self-employed crafter is you make money based on your results not on how many hours you put in. Activity doesn't count, results or profits do. Therefore, you have to make every effort count. The following time and workspace management tips will help you lower your labor costs and boost productivity by increasing the actual amount of work you can accomplish in a given time and workspace.

How to manage your time & reduce labor costs

To get the most out of your producing hours, you have to do more than organize your time. You have to have a system for handling unfinished tasks and projects. This is done through an effective follow-up system. An efficient follow-up plan changes hours that are normally wasted into profitable time.

Working more hours doesn't always mean you get more done. Working more efficiently in the time you allot for your craft business allows you to accomplish more tasks with less efforts. Here are some solutions to help you start using your time more effectively.

PROBLEM: Many of us use little post-it notes to jot down reminders of what we need to do. After writing the note we stick it on the wall or leave it on a pile on our desk or table. The problem is that we often forget to act on the notes, let them pile up in disarray, and tend to ignore them altogether. Or they get lost in the pile. Eventually the undone tasks we originally wanted to remember accumulate and production slows down. We spend additional time just trying to locate the half remembered notes.

SOLUTION: Take down all those notes from the wall and the ones lying in a pile on your worktable. Get a legal pad and write down every task and reminder, one after the other. This is your "THINGS TO DO" list. Once you have everything on one list, you are now in a position to stay on top of, to act on tasks, and to follow up. Write everything down on the list. The more projects and to-do items you put on your list, the more in charge of your time you'll be. As you accomplish a task, cross it off. What's left at the end of the day goes on the next day's list which you fill in at the end of each day.

PROBLEM: You have so many things to do, you don't know which task to do first.

SOLUTION: Set aside a little time to plan your work for the coming day or week. Schedule the morning hours for your most important jobs. Many artists report that early morning is their most creative time. Set aside routine tasks like recordkeeping or paying bills for the end of the day. This may seem simple in theory, but most of us find it's too easy to become distracted by reading the mail or talking on the phone. Meanwhile our money making projects get pushed aside. Avoid taking the time to finish the easy tasks first just to get them done and out of the way. If you do this, you won't have the energy or time to do those really important projects.

PROBLEM: The THINGS TO DO list is fine for daily tasks, but how do you keep up with what you need to do four months from now?

SOLUTION: Use a daily planner to keep track of coming show application deadlines, show dates, phone appointments and meetings. You can track everything on calendar pages or by priorities and schedule future TO DO projects. Most planners also have an address book built in to record important contact information. Another advantage is that a daily planner provides a diary of your work flow. Should you ever be audited by the IRS, a task diary is usually acceptable evidence you are engaged in a business rather than a hobby.

PROBLEM: There's too many names, too many shows, too many deadlines and too many changes to keep writing down in a calendar. And next year, you have to start again.

SOLUTION: Use a computer software program contact manager. With a contact manager, you can enter thousands of names and other data, and if there are changes, simply go in and retype the information. You can easily add customers, suppliers, and other names and important information about these folks you want to remember like family members or birthdays. You can add notes on conversations. You can create mailing labels of your customers. Contact managers have a calendar for scheduling upcoming events and reminders that pop up to tell you when you need to act. You can also prioritize your TO DO list in the computer.

How to organize your workspace & boost productivity

A cluttered workspace is psychically and emotionally draining. When you show up to work and find your production table covered with leftover materials, dust and miscellaneous notes, you experience immediate irritation and weariness. Clutter can cause you to misplace needed tools and parts. You may also misplace notifications of sales from suppliers and important show dates. You may view piles of unorganized materials as more work than there actually is to be done, thus slowing down your enthusiasm and creativity.

Organizing your work space gives you more control over your work time. Employees, if you have them, can find things if you have to leave. A tidy place to produce your crafts creates more time and lowers your cost of labor.

Disorganization is a habit. You can replace this self-defeating habit with simple, easy habits. By applying a little discipline and developing a system, you can reduce your stress level and increase your profits beginning now. It is much easier to keep everything organized than it is to sort through a mess.

Being organized and in charge of work flow creates order for spontaneity and creativity to flourish. Being organized gives you the freedom and ability to shift directions at a moment's notice.

Answering the following questionnaire at least once a year will help you learn whether your workspace is working for you or costing you hidden inconvenience and expense.

- Is your workspace adequate for your current workload?
- Is there enough lighting and ventilation?
- Do you have enough room to move around without constantly avoiding bumping into boxes or tables?
- Is there enough elbow room around your work table to produce your craftwork with ease?
- What materials, tools, patterns, and other information must you have easy access to?
- Do you find tools and equipment, family pictures, magazines and papers crowding the workspace so much that you have no place to work?
- How do you handle unfinished craft projects at the end of the day?
- Do you foresee needing a larger workspace in the near future?
- Will you have to accommodate other workers in the same space?

Obviously, much production work requires spreading out over a work space. This is not clutter. Clutter is when unrelated materials or papers end up mixed together. You can create and maintain an organized work environment by following these suggestions on a regular basis:

- Sort through materials, supplies, magazines, and books that never get used. When is the last time you used these items? Do you need them or just want them? If you haven't used materials in the past two years, consider selling them or throwing them away.

> Save trips to the post office. You can now order stamps from the U.S. Postal Service with a credit card by calling (800)782-6772. They will be mailed to you.

- Draw a diagram of your ideal workplace. Laying out parts on an assembly table puts everything within reaching distance.

- Organize your work space according to tasks. Group like things together. Ganging up pieces with similar components increases the amount of pieces you can make in a given time. Place supplies and tools for particular projects in one place.

- Hang or place tools in designated areas and return tools to their place at the end of a work day. A messy shop or office is an outward sign of an inner state of mind. Are you really in charge or are you simply responding to circumstances?

- Arrange tools and equipment so that you move from one stage of production to the next with little effort.

- Set up your operation so that you only handle materials once in any given step.

- Create a flow chart on paper of the various steps necessary to produce each item in your line. Examine your chart closely to see that all steps really flow from one to the next with minimum effort.

- If you face a massive reorganization, don't try to do it all in one day. Work methodically, taking enough time to put everything where it serves your work flow best.

- Tackle one work area at a time.

- When organizing becomes tiring, stop and rest.

- If you require additional space for storage or assembly, build or buy a building large enough to accommodate your immediate and future needs.

Some crafters insist on creating everything by means of hand tools. In this, they preserve the meaning of handcrafted. Others make use of power tools and equipment to speed the production process. A tool that reduces your labor by thirty percent will soon pay for itself many times over.

At some point in doing business, you will face the decision of upgrading equipment to increase your production output.

The test is that if sales are rising and it is clear you can only keep up with demand through purchasing needed equipment, look at your records to determine whether your current cash flow will support such a purchase. If your income won't support such a payment, you may have to seek a loan. Fortunately, loans for equipment and inventory are more easily approved because the physical equipment can be used as collateral.

Chapter 10
Tax Advantages From Your Craft Business

*"The hardest thing in the world
to understand is income tax."*
                                - Albert Einstein

In order to qualify for business deductions you have to prove your activities are based on the objective of making a profit. The test is that if you produce a profit in at least three of the last five tax years, the IRS grants that you have the intention of making a profit and therefore you are a business and not a hobby. One of the best evidence of your intentions is to keep consistent records of your business.

The following tax strategies will help you reduce taxes and save money. It is suggested you consult with an accountant about the currency of any information here.

How to lose your deductions for start-up costs

When you begin your craft business, you spend money on expenses that the IRS calls "start-up" costs. There are only two ways to deduct these costs.

One is that you capitalize the costs and get the deduction when you quit or sell your business. Obviously this is a lousy deal because how many crafters will actually sell their business?

The other way start-up costs can be deducted is to amortize or spread out the deductions over five years. But you must choose to do this in the start-up year.

It is important in the beginning of your business to make the right choice. If you don't make the correct choice, you may lose your deductions.

For instance, say you spent $7,000 on equipment, tools, furniture, travel, and rent to start-up a craft business which as of yet does not exist. You deduct these expenses from your income as normal business expenses. The IRS disallows your deductions because the business did not exist when you put that money out. By this time, you are into the next tax year. You lose the chance to amortize and must now wait until you sell or quit the business.

To get your deduction, choose to amortize these costs in the tax year during which the active business starts. Consult an accountant. Start-up costs are any money paid to create an active business and any expenses that would normally be deductible if there were an existing business. Examples include travel, entertainment, hiring consultants, advertising, training, finding suppliers, finding buyers, getting professional accounting advice, tools, and so on.

Avoid IRS audits

Use a daily planner or appointment book and record your business activities every day. Keep receipts for all expenses and sales, canceled checks, credit card charge slips, letters, photographs, and any additional evidence to support your claims. The way the tax law reads, it is a requirement to keep a diary of daily tasks to prove business activity. In 1995, it became tax law that you are not required to keep receipts for business travel and entertainment expenses less than $75 while out of town.

As for as receipts, keep them all. Canceled checks are not enough alone, as you have to produce documentation to list your expenses.

Use a separate credit card for business costs because you get a receipt as proof of payment and you get a monthly statement as proof of payment. If you make a charge for a business expense near the end of the year, it will be deductible in the year charged. A separate charge card for business also allows you to track business interest payments which is deductible.

Some of the documentation proofs that may safeguard you from an audit include an appointment book, a business customer list, a daily log or receipts, journal of expenses and income, deposit slips, bank statements, and canceled checks. Another tip, make sure your receipts match your claims. An auditor can check your motel receipts to show how many people occupied the room.

If your children drive your car, their signature on credit card receipts indicates use by family rather than business. Unless you prove you have them on the payroll doing work for you at the time.

Your auto repair bills will often indicate mileage. Make sure your mileage claims for business use of your car match repair receipts.

Here's additional preparatory advice to help avoid audits:

√   Mail your tax return by registered mail, requesting a return receipt.

√   Mail your return a day before the due date.

√   Write your registered mail receipt number on your original return before you copy and mail to the IRS.

√   Add statements, copies of checks, appraisals, police reports, etc. for any casualty claims.

√   Notify IRS of address change.

√   File on time.

√   Have a tax advisor, like a C.P.A., sign your return.

√   Report all your income.

√   Don't claim illegitimate deductions.

√   Don't ever claim more than 14 withholding allowances.

√   Answer audit questions in advance and better your chances of avoiding an audit. You can see the *IRS Audit Manual* at your tax advisor's office.

Dealing with the IRS

There are two types of IRS employees that will examine your returns. The first is called a tax auditor. A tax auditor is required to have four year college degree in any field, not necessarily accounting. They advance through the ranks by completing basic bookkeeping courses. Tax auditors are not experts in tax law. They look at your receipts, compare them to your returns, and then tell you if you are short. You can probably handle this kind of interview without the presence of your accountant. However, you should consult your accountant before the appointment.

The second type of IRS employee is a revenue agent. They have four year college degrees and a minimum of 24 semester hours of accounting education. The revenue agent is familiar with IRS tax law. If your appointment is with a revenue agent, you should be accompanied by a tax advisor who understands IRS and agent's language.

Getting the most out of your home office deductions

You can use many structures for your home office business. Examples include a house, apartment, condo, mobile home, or boat. You can also include structures on property like a separate garage, studio, barn, or greenhouse. The home office deduction is probably worth about $1,000 in deductions for each $100,000 in home worth. The IRS considers your home office as your principal place of business when you:

√   Use it for performing the important functions of your business.

√   Collect money from customers in it.

√   Spend more time in the home office than at other work locations.

You can deduct expenses for a separate structure like a studio or garage if the building is used exclusively for the business. In this case, the building does not have to be the principal place of business or a place where you meet customers.

You can also expense property or assets used for your business in your home, even if you don't qualify for the home office deduction. For instance, you buy a new work table that costs $500. Your home business does not qualify you for home office deduction because you use the room only 75% for the business (you must use the room 100% for business to qualify.) You can expense $375 of the table or 75% of $500.

You are allowed to deduct up to $17,500 of the cost of new or used office equipment, tools and other qualifying personal property bought in the same tax year. You must use the property 100% for business or you can only deduct the percentage of business use of the property. Also you can only deduct up to the amount of business income for the same tax year. Any cost chosen to be expensed that is above the limitation of the current year can be carried into the next year.

You can deduct indirect expenses like rent, utilities, insurance, security systems, property taxes, deductible mortgage interest, repairs, and depreciation in proportion to your business use of the home. To determine the amount, first find out the total square feet of your home. Then measure the square feet of your home office.

Divide the home office footage by the total area of the house. That gives you the percentage to multiply your indirect expenses by.

Say you have a 1,600 square foot house and you use one 400 square foot room for business. You use 25% of your home for business and can deduct 25% of the indirect expenses. Remember to keep a journal or diary proving this room is only used for business. Photos with dates stamped by the film developers will be acceptable evidence.

Hire your kids as employees

If your child is over six years old, the IRS says they may be a real employee. If the child is under eighteen years old, wages parents pay their children are a legitimate deduction. You can't use your children as employees if your business is a corporation or a partnership, only if you are a sole proprietorship, independent contractor, or an employee. To qualify the deduction must be:

√   A reasonable amount.
√   Paid for services actually performed.
√   Actually paid.

Your child's employment must be by the books and you have to prove it with check stubs, receipts, and a diary. Use a time sheet like on the following page to record hours worked and tasks accomplished.

You benefit from hiring a child under eighteen, because you can deduct wages, which reduces your income and self-employment taxes. However, you have to prove that the amount you pay in wages is a normal wage for the particular tasks and not artificially high.

Figure 10.1, Time Sheet for employees

Time Sheet		
Employee Name:		
Date	Work Description	Hours
4/27/97	stuffed envelopes for mailing 200 catalogs	4
4/28/97	delivered packages to post office	1/2
4/28/97	made copies of new flyer	1
4/29/97	cleaned van for show trip	3

You can lease equipment from children over 18

Say that you give your daughter equipment like a car you have already completely depreciated and it has a fair market value of $5,000. Your daughter then rents the car to your company for $100 a month for five years.

You get to deduct $1,200 a year from equipment you would normally have gotten zero deduction from because it is already depreciated. Your daughter has to report $1,200 income, but she is probably in a lower income bracket anyway. To meet the conditions for such a lease, you must:

√   Give up control of the equipment.
√   Put the lease in writing.
√   Make the rental amount reasonable.
√   Prove you really need the equipment in the business.

Save money by leasing from your spouse

Since rent is a deductible business expense, you pay Social Security and self-employment taxes on your net business income after you deduct any rent you pay to your spouse.

You report rent income (your spouse's) on Schedule E of your tax return where you deduct depreciation. On rental income, you don't pay Social Security of self-employment taxes.

When husband and wife are separate taxpayers, rent paid by the husband to the wife, or vice versa, is deductible by the husband and reportable income for the wife, or vice versa.

If your business income is under $61,000, for each dollar of rent expense you claim, you will save around 15%.

Possible assets you might need in your business you could rent from your spouse include a car, desk, computer, tools, furniture, office equipment, and even office or studio space. The test is do you really need it in your business and would you rent it from a retail rental agent? To pass an audit for claiming the rent from spouse, you must prove that:

√   You paid fair market rent for the assets.
√   You have a written agreement.
√   Your spouse received payments and deposited them in a separate account.
√   Your spouse can prove they owned the assets.
√   You paid state sales tax on the rentals.

Hire your spouse and get 100% write off of medical expenses

Self-employed health deduction allows you to deduct 30% of money spent on health insurance. You would get a much better deal by hiring your spouse and paying medical expenses under an employee health plan. You can then claim 100% of those expenses as a deductible employee expenses on your Schedule C.

Getting the most out of automobile deductions

A trip from your home to your office or any regular place of business is considered commuting, therefore personal, and not deductible as a business expense. However, you can deduct miles driven between two business locations. So if you have a home office and you drive to a store account, that is legitimate deductible mileage. For 2002, the standard mileage deduction was 36 cents per business mile. This rate changes year to year, so be sure to check your IRS booklet for the current rate.

You can claim the IRS standard mileage or figure all your gas, repairs, tires, oil, insurance, registration fees, and depreciation.

You must have adequate records to prove your total miles driven during the tax year. Break down the mileage into business use, commuting, and personal use.

Turning travel and entertainment into business deductions

You can claim travel expenses for your business if you have to spend the night away from home while pursuing business. Even if you spend some time for personal reasons, as long as you spend more days on business than pleasure, deduct 100% of travel

Figure 10.2, Mileage Log

MILEAGE LOG				
DATE	BEGINNING MILEAGE	ENDING MILEAGE	TOTAL MILES DRIVEN	REASON FOR TRIP
8/5/97	45670	45699	29	PICK UP SHELVES
8/7/97	45699	45809	110	PHOENIX SHOW
8/9/97	45809	45812	3	POST OFFICE

expenses. For each day of business travel, deduct lodging costs, and 50% of your meals. If weather or other circumstances prevent you from carrying out your business, you can still deduct the travel expenses.

You can deduct travel costs to attend trade shows, trainings and conventions if business related. If your spouse or children are employed by you, you can deduct their expenses, too.

Your travel expense deductions are more credible if you log and record the expenses at the time of purchase. Usually, taxpayers who lose court cases involving travel lacked proper entries in a diary. You should record:

√ Amount you spent on lodging, food, gas, parking, or taxis.
√ Time of day you departed and returned for each trip and number of days away for business.
√ Place you traveled to.
√ Nature of business or purpose of business trip.

Here are the categories of expenses for travel recognized by the IRS:

√ Meals and lodgings, both on the way to and at the business destination.
√ Transportation costs like air, train, or bus and any costs of transporting baggage, samples, or display materials.
√ Operation and maintenance costs of automobiles, trailers, or airplanes.
√ Laundry and cleaning if you dirty your clothes while traveling.
√ Telephone expenses.
√ Taxi or bus charges between an airport or station and lodging or place of business plus any tips.

When you are documenting entertainment expenses, you must document or lose the deduction:

√   Who you entertained.

√   Why you paid for entertainment or what business benefit was expected.

√   Where the entertainment happened.

√   When, by date and time.

√   How much you spent.

The tax tips presented in this chapter will give you several ways to cut your tax costs and save you money. Consult your C.P.A. before applying any of the suggestions here because tax laws change every year.

A reference for additional money saving strategies is *422 Tax Deductions* by Bernard Kamoroff, C.P.A.

Make money selling your crafts on the internet. The new book by James Dillehay, *The Basic Guide to Selling Crafts on the Internet* ($16.95) can be ordered from 1-800-235-6570. Also see *The Directory of Grants for Crafts* ($14.95). For more details, visit www.craftmarketer.com

Appendix A
Recordkeeping Forms

The following forms are blank versions of examples throughout the book. You can photocopy and enlarge them for your own use or use them as models to create your own forms.

ACCOUNTS PAYABLE

DATE	INVOICE #	VENDOR	DUE DATE	AMT. CHARGE	AMT. PAID
				ENDING BALANCE	

ACCOUNTS RECEIVABLE

DATE	INVOICE #	CUSTOMER	DUE DATE	AMT. CHARGE	AMT. PAID
				ENDING BALANCE	

BALANCE SHEET as of: _____		
ASSETS		
	Current Assets	
	Checking/Savings Accounts	
	Accounts Receivable	
	Inventory Assets	
	Consigned Inventory Assets	
	Fixed Assets	
	Land	
	Buildings	
	Equipment	
	Furniture	
	Vehicles	
	Other Assets	
	Total Current Assets	
LIABILITIES		
	Current Liabilities	
	Accounts Payable	
	Notes Payable, due within one year	
	TAXES PAYABLE	
	Federal Income Tax	
	State Income Tax	
	Self Employment Tax	
	Sales Tax	
	Long Term Liabilities	
	Total Liabilities	
	OWNER'S EQUITY	

CASH IN for: _____	
BEGINNING CASH ON HAND	
SALES-INCOME	
OTHER INCOME	
interest	
SALES OF ASSETS	
LOANS	
PERSONAL INVESTMENT	
TOTAL CASH IN	

CASH OUT for: _____	
START UP COSTS	
business permits/licenses	
other	
DIRECT COSTS	
labor	
materials	
freight	
miscellaneous	
TOTAL DIRECT COSTS	
INDIRECT EXPENSES	
rent	
utilities	
insurance	
phone	
travel	
miscellaneous	
TOTAL INDIRECT COSTS	
ASSETS	
long term purchases	
DEBTS OR LIABILITIES	
loan payments	
OWNER'S SALARY	
TOTAL CASH OUT	

CASH FLOW for: _____

	IN-FLOW	OUT-FLOW	BALANCE
BEG. CASH BALANCE			
expenses			
sales			
weekly to date total			
expenses			
sales			
weekly to date total			
expenses			
sales			
weekly to date total			
expenses			
sales			
weekly to date total			
CASH ON HAND			

DEPRECIATION for _____

Date purchased or first used	
Description	
Method of depreciation	
Depreciation schedule	
Percent used for business	
Cost	
Balance to be depreciated	
Depreciated _____ (yr)	
Balance to be depreciated	
Depreciated _____ (yr)	
Balance to be depreciated	
Depreciated _____ (yr)	
Balance to be depreciated	
Depreciated _____ (yr)	
Balance to be depreciated	
Depreciated _____ (yr)	
Balance to be depreciated	
Depreciated _____ (yr)	
Balance to be depreciated	
Depreciated _____ (yr)	

INVENTORY:

DATE	SOLD TO:	UNITS MADE	UNITS SOLD	BALANCE ON HAND

MILEAGE LOG				
DATE	BEGINNING MILEAGE	ENDING MILEAGE	TOTAL MILES DRIVEN	REASON FOR TRIP

PROFIT & LOSS INCOME STATEMENT			
INCOME			
	TOTAL INCOME		
	Cost of Goods Sold		
	GROSS PROFIT		
EXPENSES			
	TOTAL EXPENSES		
NET INCOME (before taxes)			

PRO-FORMA INCOME STATEMENT
ONE-YEAR PROJECTION

INCOME		
	Net Sales	
	Cost of Goods Sold	
	Gross Profit	
EXPENSES		
	Indirect Expenses	
INCOME FROM OPERATIONS		
	Other Income	
	Other Expenses	
NET PROFIT/LOSS before taxes		
TAXES		
	Federal Income Tax	
	State Income Tax	
	Social Security	
NET PROFIT/LOSS after taxes		

PROFIT FOR: _____

Market	Price	Productio-n Cost	Cost of Sales	Profit

PROFIT/VOLUME
FOR: _____

Market	Units Sold	Profit	Total Volume

TELEPHONE LOG				
DATE	TIME	WHO CALLED	LENGTH	COST

TIME SHEET

Employee Name:

Date	Work Description	Hours

TRAVEL & ENTERTAINMENT LOG				
DATE	LOCATION	REASON	CLIENT	COST

WEEKLY EXPENSE RECORD				
Acct	INDIRECT EXPENSES	Total this week	Total up to week	Total to date
	Mdse/materials			
	Accounting			
	Advertising			
	Auto expense			
	Contributions			
	Licenses			
	Misc. expenses			
	Office			
	Postage			
	Rent			
	Repairs			
	SUBTOTAL			
	TOTAL THIS WEEK			
	UP TO THIS WEEK			
	TOTAL TO DATE			

WEEKLY INCOME RECORD Week Ending:			
DAY	TOTAL RECEIPTS FROM BUSINESS		AMOUNT
SUN			
MON			
TUES			
WED			
THUR			
FRI			
SAT			
TOTAL THIS WEEK			
TOTAL UP TO THIS WEEK			
TOTAL TO DATE			

WEEKLY PAYROLL RECORD

		DEDUCTIONS				
EMPLOYE-E	TOTAL WAGES	SOC. SEC.	MED.	FED. INC. TAX	OTHER	PAID

Appendix B
Lead SBDC Offices

Take advantage of free and low cost business training at Small Business Development Centers. Contact these central offices to find the local center nearest you.

University of Alaska -- SBDC
430 West 7th Ave Ste 110
Anchorage AK 99501
907-274-7232

SBDC / University of Alabama
Alabama Tech Assist Program
1717 11th Ave S Suite 419
Birmingham AL 35294
205-934-7260

Arkansas SBDC
University of Arkansas
Little Rock Tech. Cent. Bldg.
100 S. Main Ste. 401
Little Rock AR 72201
501-324-9043

Arizona SBDC
9215 N. Black Canyon Hghwy
Phoenix AZ 85021
602-943-9818

Greater Sacromento SBDC
1787 Tribute Rd Ste A
Sacramento CA 95815
916-263-6580

Colorado SBDC
Office of Economic
Development
1625 Broadway Ste 1710
Denver CO 80202
303-892-3809

University of Connecticut
SBDC -- Box U-41 Rm 422
368 Fairfield Rd
Storrs CT 06269
203-486-4135

District of Columbia SBDC
Howard University
2600 6th St Rm 128
Washington DC 20059
202-806-1550

Delaware SBDC
Univ. of Delaware
Purnell Hall Suite 005
Newark DE 19716
302-831-1555

Florida SBDC Network
Univ. of West Florida
19 W Garden St #300
Pensacola FL 32501
904-444-2060

Georgia SBDC
University of Georgia
Chicopee Complex
1180 East Broad St
Athens GA 30602
706-542-6762

Hawaii SBDC
Univ. of Hawaii at Hilo
200 W Kawili St
Hilo HI 96720
808-933-3515

Iowa SBDC
Iowa State University
State Administrative Office
137 Lynn Ave
Ames IA 50010
515-292-6351

Idaho SBDC
Boise State University
College of Business
1910 Univ. Drive
Boise ID 83725
208-385-1640

Illinois SBDC Network
Dept. of Commerce
620 East Adams St 6th Flr
Springfield IL 62701
217-524-5856

Indiana SBDC
Economic Devpt. Council
One North Capitol Ste 420
Indianapolis IN 46204
317-264-6871

Wichita State Univ. - SBDC
1845 Fairmount
Wichita KS 67260
316-689-3193

Kentucky SBDC -
University of Kentucky
Center for Business Dvlp
College of Business
225 Business & Eco. Bldg.
Lexington KY 40506
606-257-7668

Louisiana SBDC
Northeast Louisiana Univ.
Adm. 2-57
Monroe LA 71209
318-342-5506

Massachusetts SBDC
Univ. of Massachusetts
205 School of Management
Amherst MA 01003
413-545-6301

Maryland SBDC
Dept. of Econ. & Emp. Dvlpt.
217 E. Redwood St 10th Flr.
Baltimore MD 21202
410-767-6552

Maine SBDC
Univ. of Southern Maine
99 Falmouth St.
Portland ME 04103
207-780-4420

Wayne State Univ. -- SBDC
2727 Second Ave Ste 121
Detroit MI 48201
313-577-4850

MN SBDC Dept. of Trade
900 American Center Bldg.
150 East Kellogg Blvd.
St. Paul MN 55101
612-297-5770

Missouri SBDC
Univ. of Missouri, Suite 300
1800 University Place
Columbia MO 65211
573-882-7096

Mississippi SBDC
Univ. of Mississippi
Old Chemistry Bldg Suite 216
University MS 38677
601-232-5001

Montana SBDC
Dept. of Commerce
1424 Ninth Ave.
Helena MT 59620
406-444-4392

Missoula SBDC
MT W Region Econ Dev Grp
127 N. Higgins 3rd Flr.
Missoula MT 59802
406-728-9234

North Carolina SBDC
333 Fayetteville St Mall #1150
Raleigh NC 27601
919-715-7272

North Dakota SBDC
Univ. of North Dakota
118 Gamble Hall Box 7308
Gtand Forks ND 58202
701-777-3700

Univ. of Nebraska at Omaha
SBDC -- Peter Keiwit
Conference Cntr.
1313 Farnam Ste 132
Omaha NE 68182
402-595-2381

New Hampshire SBDC
Univ. of New Hampshire
108 McConnnell Hall
Durham NH 03824
603-862-2200

Rutgers\State University of NJ at
Camden
SBDC -- University Heights
180 University Ave 3rd Flr.
Newark NJ 07102
201-648-5950

New Mexico SBDC
Sante Fe Community College
PO Box 4187
Sante Fe NM 87502
505-438-1362

Nevada SBDC
Univ. of Nevada at Reno
Col. of Bus. Admn. Rm. 411
Reno NV 89577
702-784-1717

New York SBDC
State Univ. of New York
State University Plaza
Albany NY 12246
518-443-5398

Ohio SBDC
Department of Development
State Office Tower
PO Box 1001
Columbus OH 43226
614-644-8748

SE State Univ. SBDC
517 University
Durant OK 74701
405-924-0277

Oregon SBDC
44 W Broadway Ste 501
Eugene OR 97401
541-726-2250

Pennsylvania SBDC
University of Pennsylvania
The Wharton School
444 Vance Hall
3733 Spruce St
Philadelphia PA 19104
215-898-1219

Rhode Island SBDC
Bryant College
1150 Douglas Pike
Smithfield RI 02917
401-232-6111

South Carolina SBDC
Univ. of South Carolina
College of Bus. Admin.
Columbia SC 29201
803-777-5118

Univ. of South Dakota -- SBDC
School of Business Rm 115
414 East Clark
Vermillion SD 57069
605-677-5498

Tenessee SBDC
Memphis State Univ.
South Campus Bldg. 1
Memphis TN 38152
901-678-2500

North Texas SBDC
Dallas Cty Community College
1402 Corinth Street
Dallas TX 75215
214-860-5831

Houston SBDC
Univ. of Houston
1100 Louisiana Ste 500
Houston TX 77002
713-752-8400

Northwest Texas SBDC
Spectrum Plaza
2579 South Loop 289 # 114
Lubbock TX 79423
806-745-3973

South Texas Border SBDC
UTSA Downtown
1222 N Main Ste 450
San Antonio TX 78212
210-558-2450

Utah SBDC
Univ. of Utah
102 West 500 South #315
Salt Lake City UT 84101
801-581-7905

Virginia SBDC
PO Box 798
Richmond VA 23206
804-371-8253

Washington SBDC
Washington State Univ.
245 Todd Hall
Pullman WA 99164
509-335-1576

Wisconsin SBDC
Univ. of Wisconsin
432 N. Lake Street Room 423
Madison WI 53706
608-263-7794

West Virginia SBDC - WV
Development Office
1115 Virginia Street East
Capitol Complex
Charleston WV 25310
304-558-2960

Univ. of Wyoming - SBDC
PO Box 3275
University Station
Laramie WY 82070
307-766-2363

Index

About the Author

James Dillehay is a professional craft artist, writer, and educator of 19 years experience. Author of seven books, Dillehay's craft marketing articles have helpd readers of *Family Circle, The National Examiner, The Crafts Report, Better Homes & Gardens: Crafting for Profit, Sunshine Artist, Ceramics Monthly, Florida Retirement Lifestyles* and many more publications. He was a featured guest on The Carol Duvall Show, HGTV. His book, *The Basic Guide to Selling Arts and Crafts*, was included in the training program of the Association of Creative Craft Industries (ACCI). James is a member of the advisory boards to the National Craft Association and ArtisanStreet.com. He was listed in the 1998 *Who's Who of American Entrepreneurs.*

James lives in the Manzano Mountains of New Mexico. He teaches and speaks nationally on how to achieve craft business success. If you have questions about marketing your crafts, visit the discussion group at www.craftmarketer.com to get answers.

For a free email newsletter with tips and news about craft business, visit www.craftmarketer.com

Craft Business Books Catalog

The Basic Guide to Selling Arts & Crafts by James Dillehay. Gives step-by-step help on over 150 topics. Find the best fairs, sell to stores, get interior designers and corporations to buy your work, make money from spin-off ideas, sell your crafts mail order, discover overlooked markets, what to do when your work isn't selling. Appendixes list over 250 sources and reference books for the artisan. This book was used as the professional crafters training manual by the Association of Creative Craft Industries. Softcover, 6"x9", 196 pages, softcover, illustrations, index, $14.95

The Basic Guide to Selling Crafts On the Internet by James Dillehay. Discover how the Internet can help you sell more of your craftwork and lower your marketing costs. Includes using a web site, search engines, email, discussion groups, online auctions, publicity, advertising and hundreds of more tips. Learn how to effectively track results of your promotions to see what's working and what isn't. Resources include sites to get free advertising, free graphics and software, free web pages, free tutorials on web design for business, online media contacts, free newsletters and newsgroups about your craft and internet marketing. Softcover, 6"x9", 168 pages, charts, index, $16.95

The Basic Guide to Pricing Your Craftwork by James Dillehay. One of the most often asked questions from craftpersons selling their work is *"How much should I charge?"* Whether you are a seasoned professional or just starting, this guide will give you the tools to beome more profitable and competitive. You will learn basic formulas for pricing your craftwork in selling retail or wholesale, how to use pricing strategies to increase sales, how to increase the perceived value of your products, how to know if you are really making a profit, how to keep records, and how to manage your time and workspace to reduce your labor costs and boost productivity. Your success as a professional crafter may very well depend on what you find in this guide. Softcover, 140 pages, 6"x9", illustrated, charts, index, $12.95

Directory of Grants for Crafts and How to Write a Winning Proposal by James Dillehay. Learn everything you need to know about locating and getting free money through grants from foundations, corporations and the government. Learn how to draft a grant proposal and fill in grant applications. Learn how to follow the grant process from planning to submitting. This guide includes over 1,000 listings, contact information and subject areas of grants available for artists and crafts persons. Softcover, 214 pages, 6"x9", index, $14.95

Guerrilla Marketing for Artists and Craftspersons by James Dillehay and Jay Conrad Levinson. How will your art or craft stand out from the others? Take your business to the top with the Best-selling Marketing Series in History and get new customers with the best low-cost marketing program available. The marketplace is more competitive today than at any other time in history. This course is essential if you want to succeed. You will get solid, practical, cost-effective tactics on how to take advantage of the most recent advances in marketing. These advances could save your business and give you an all-important competitive edge. Forthcoming in Spring 2004.

Order these books at **www.craftmarketer.com**
or call toll-free at **1-800-235-6570**